CALMING MANDALAS FOR STRESS RELIEF

COLORING BOOK

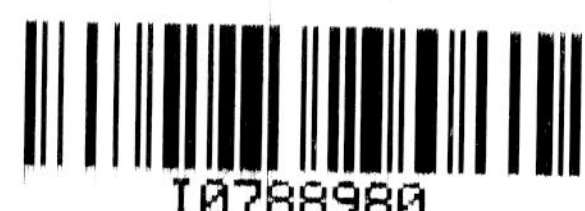

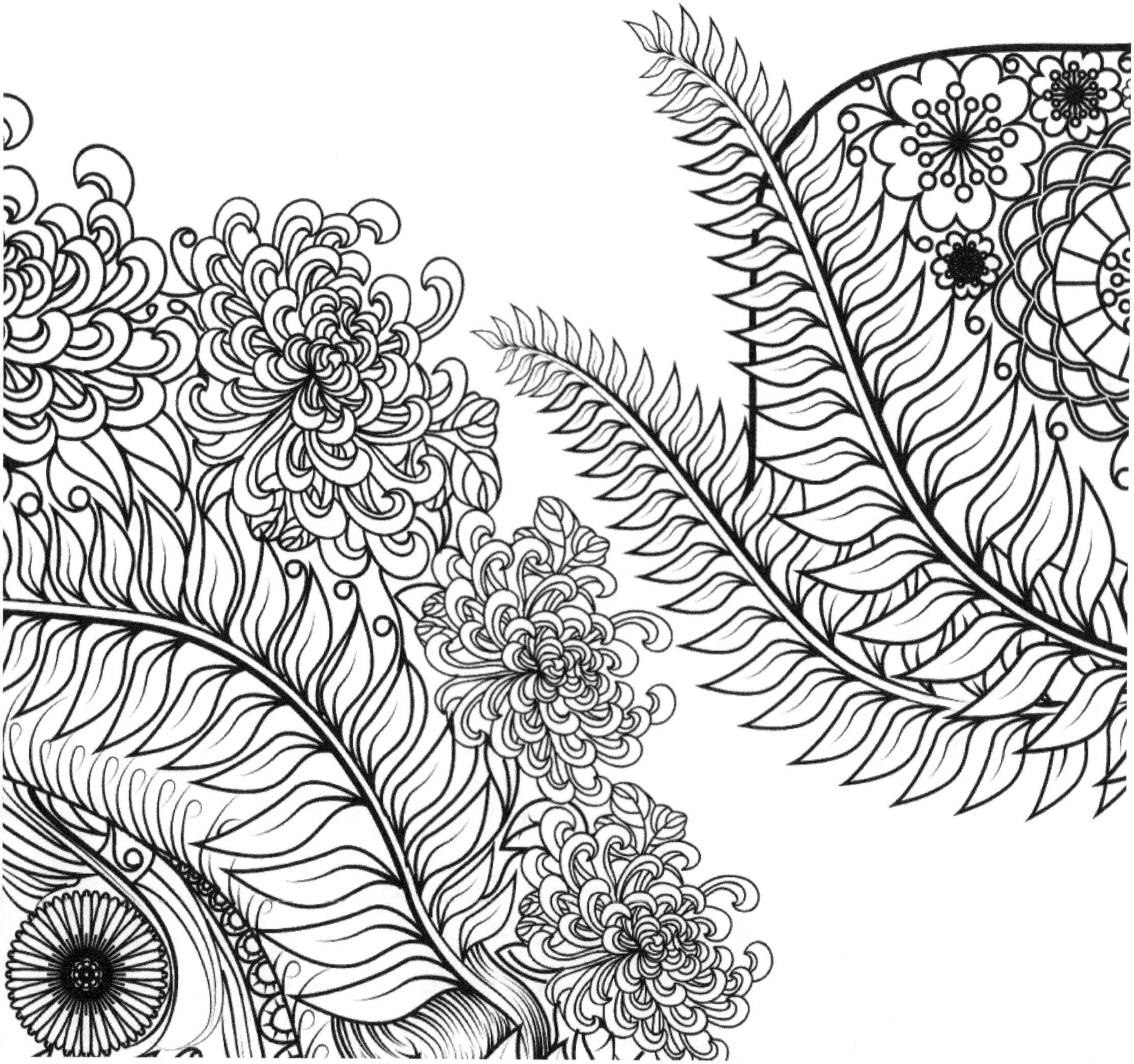

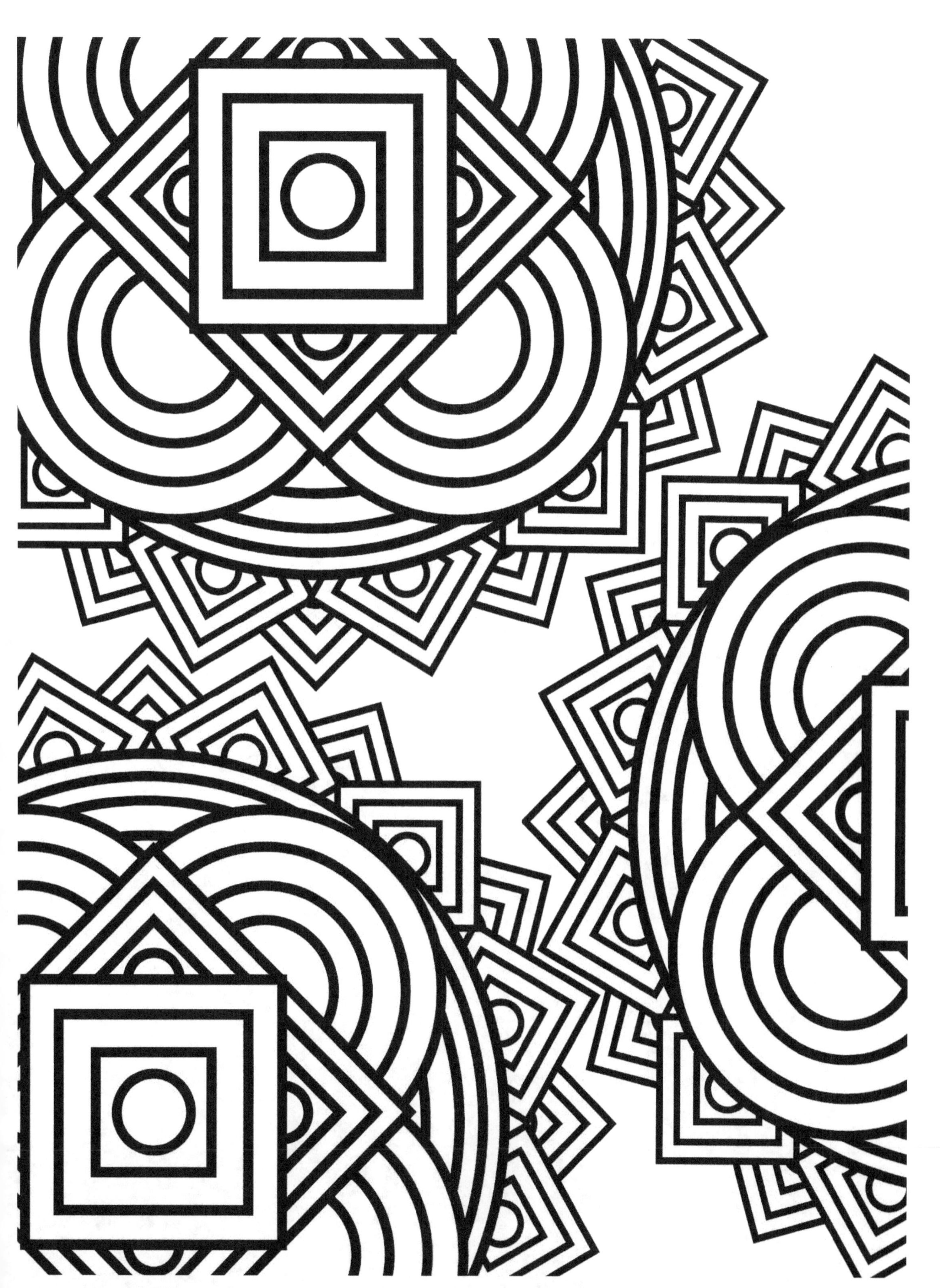

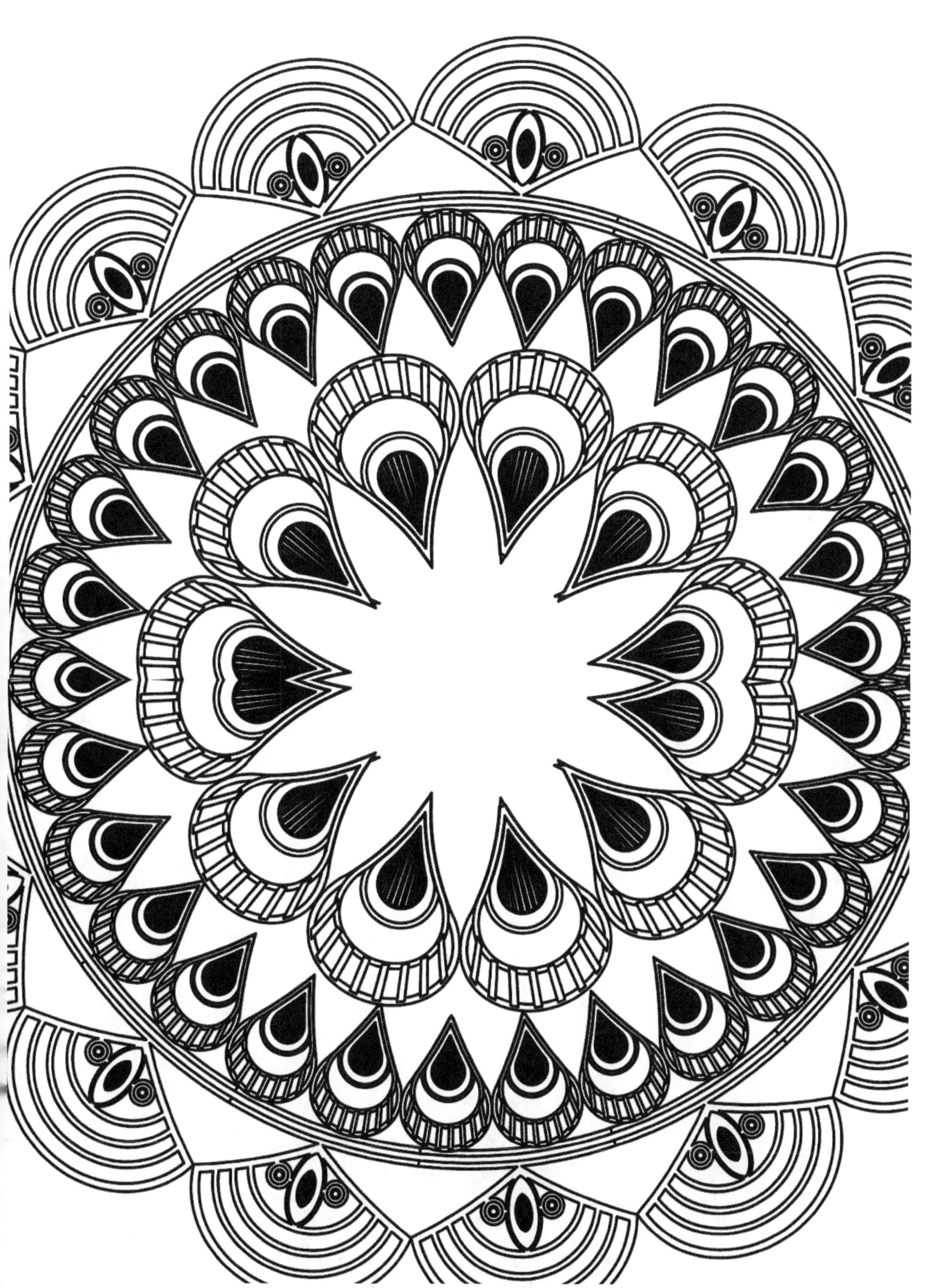

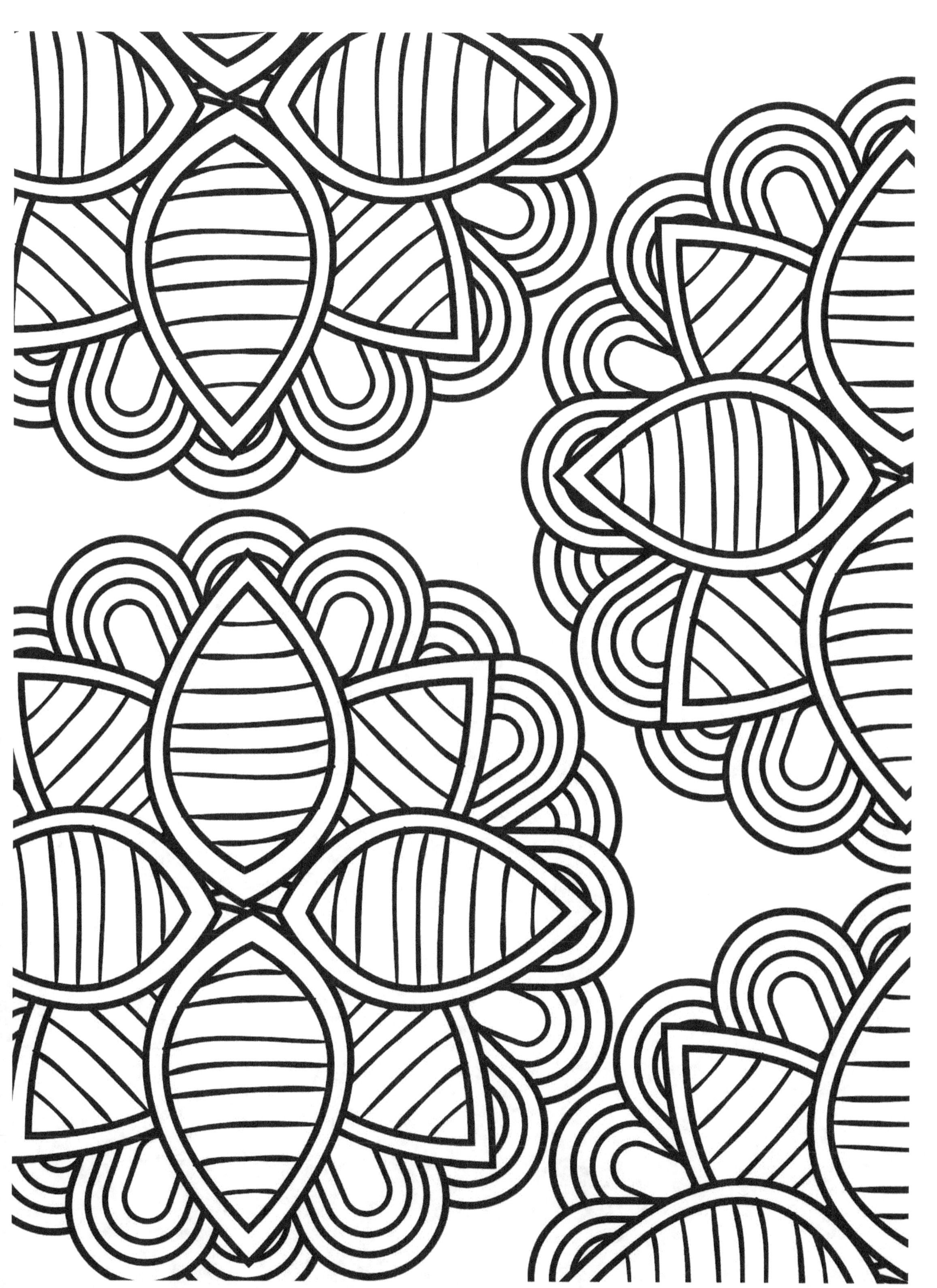

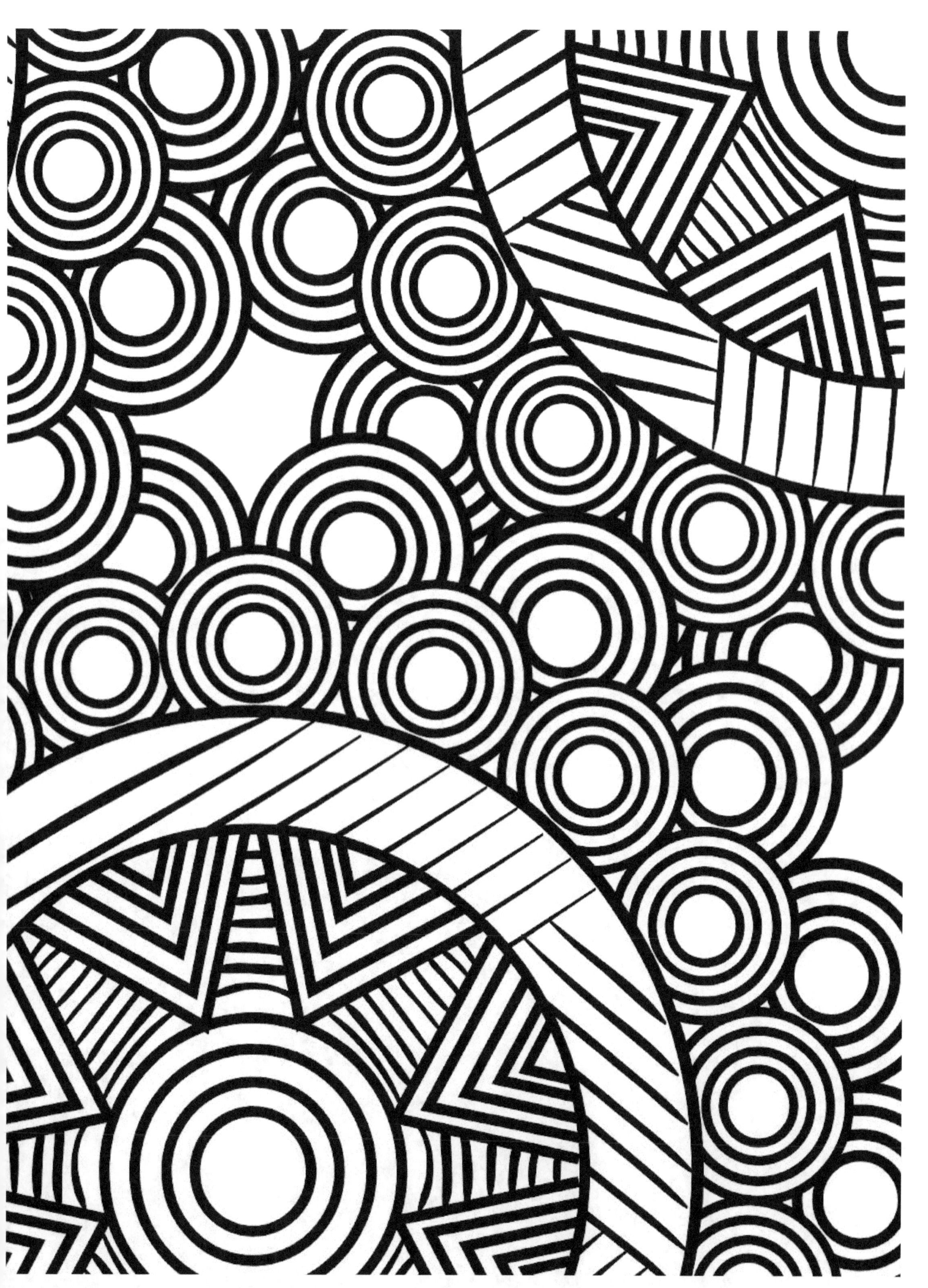

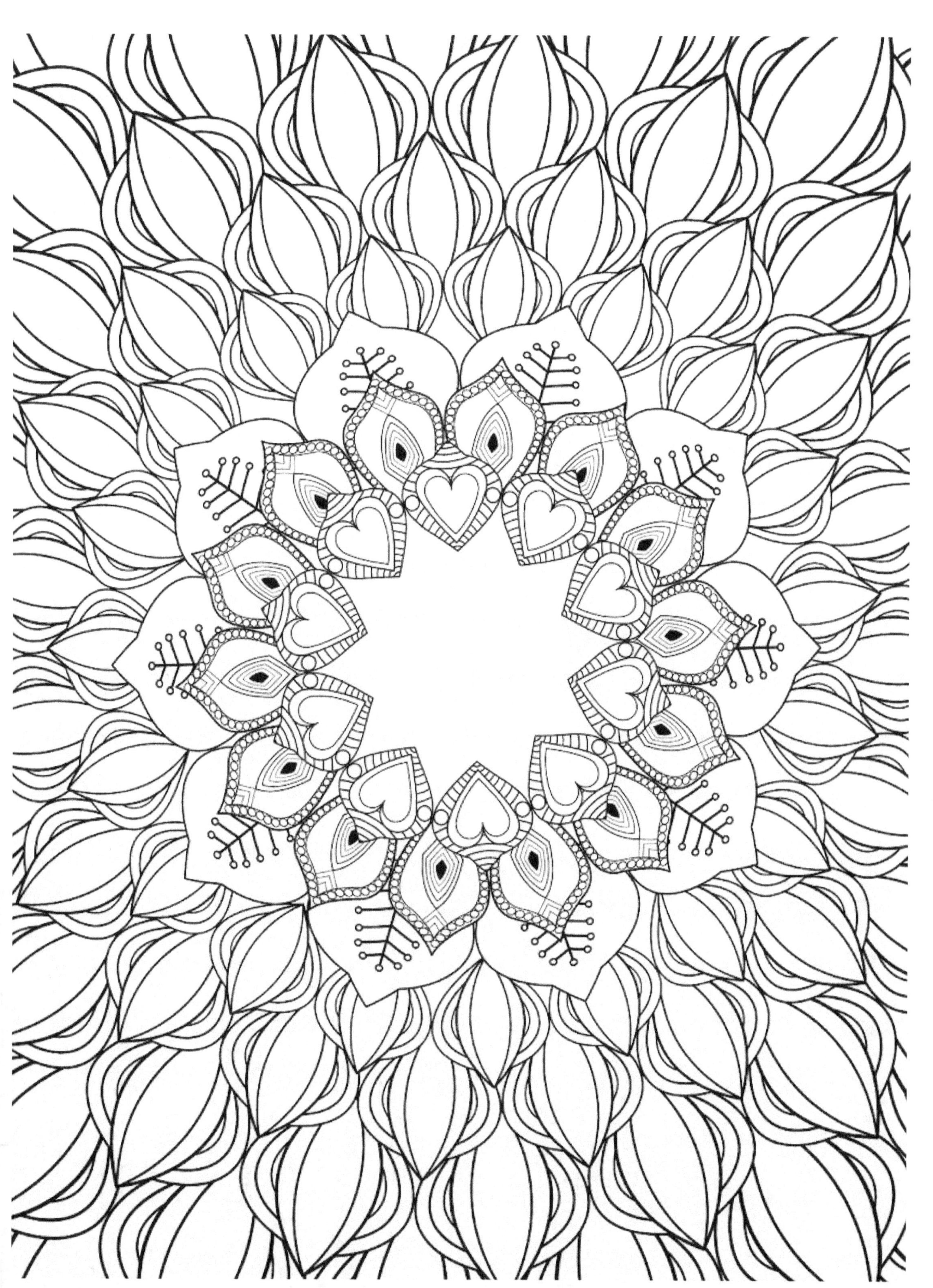

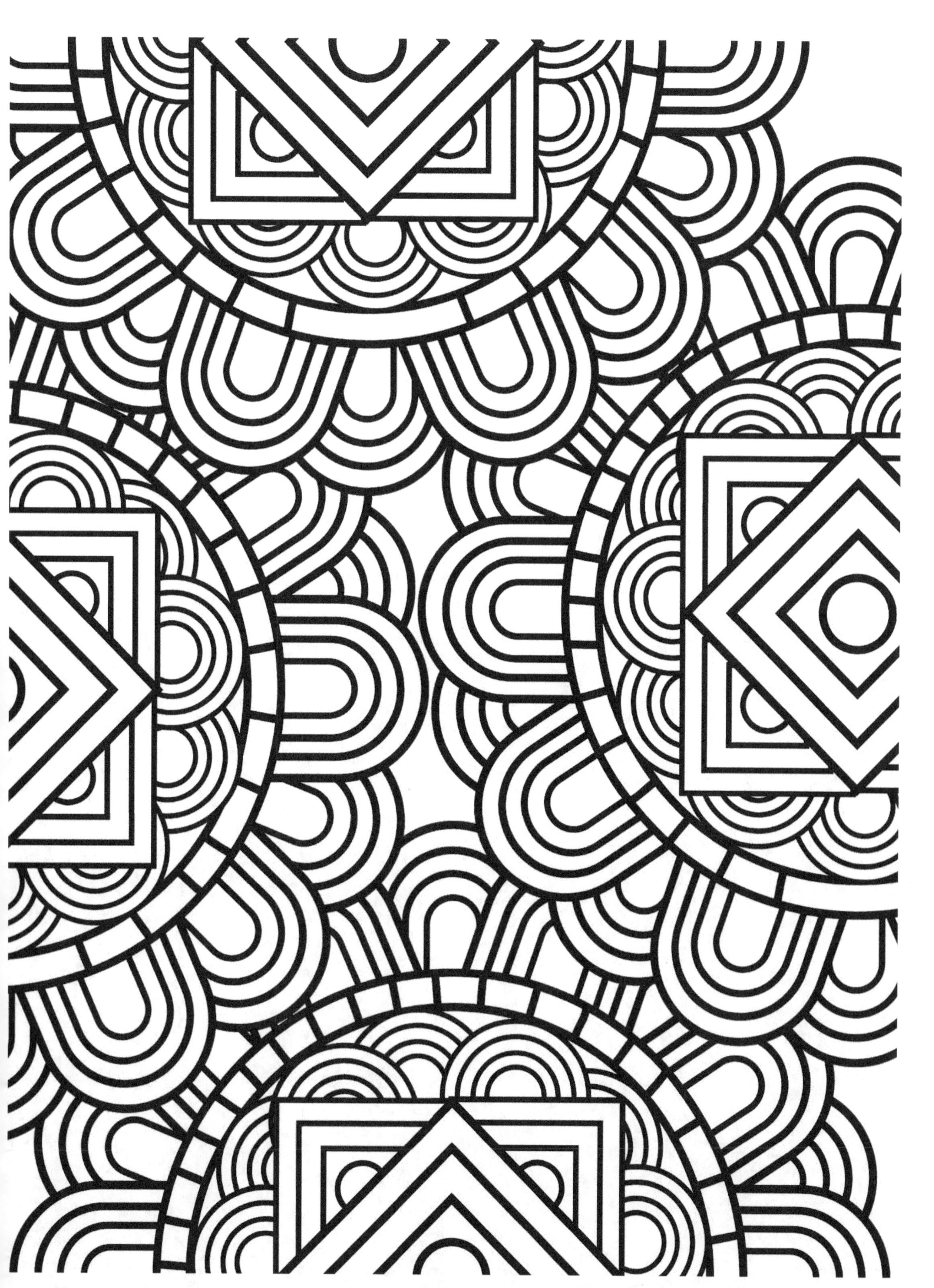

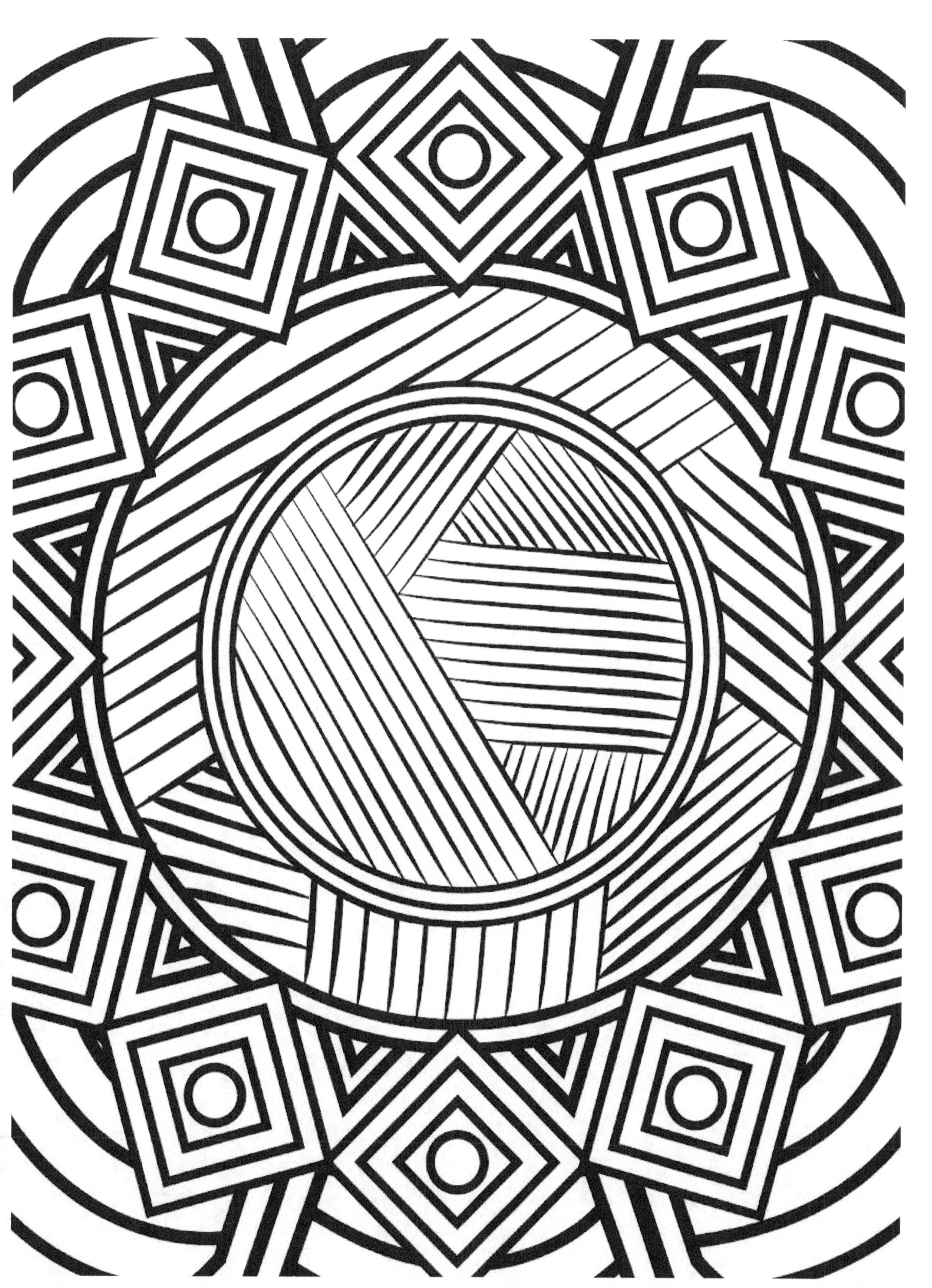

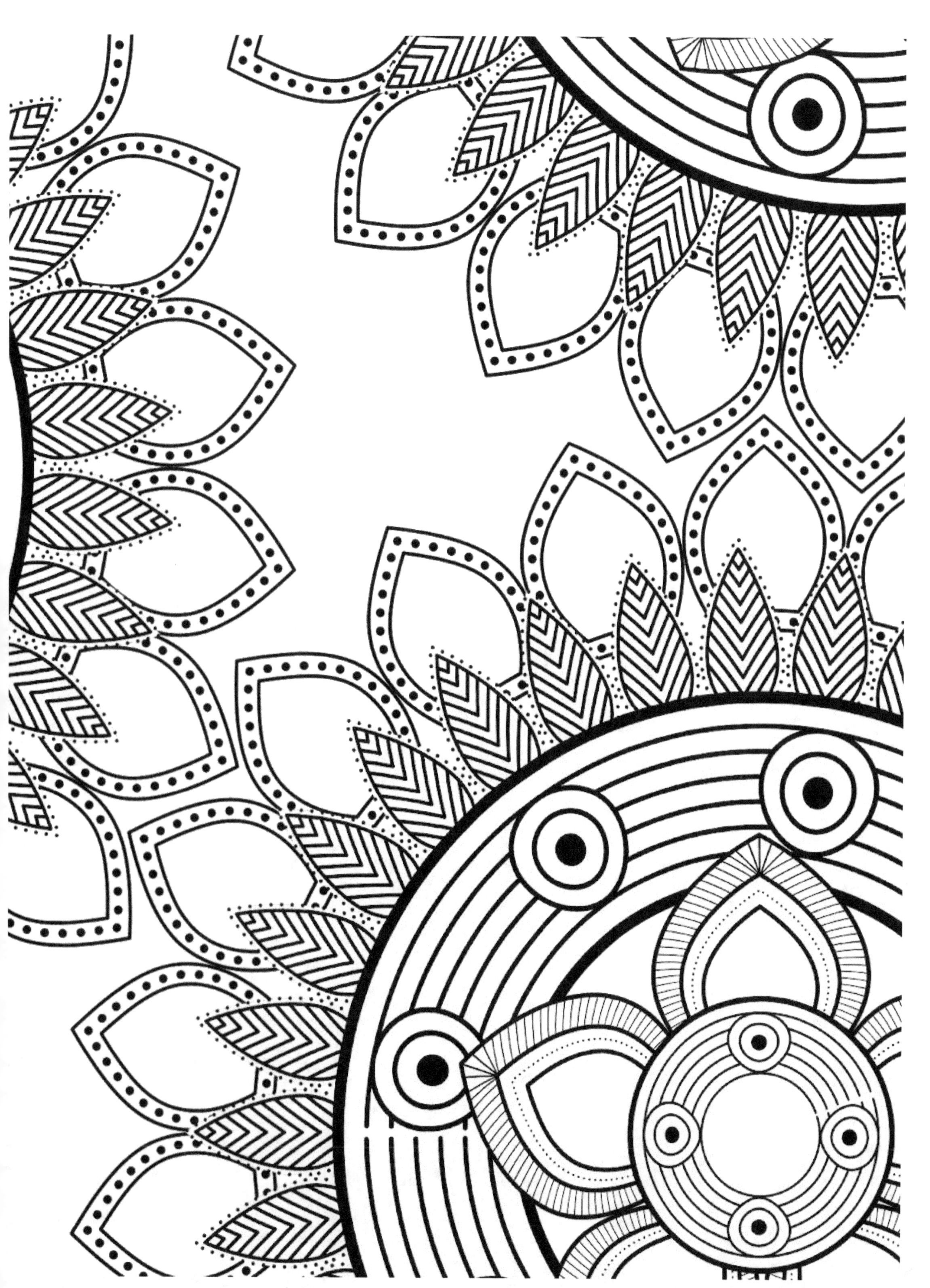

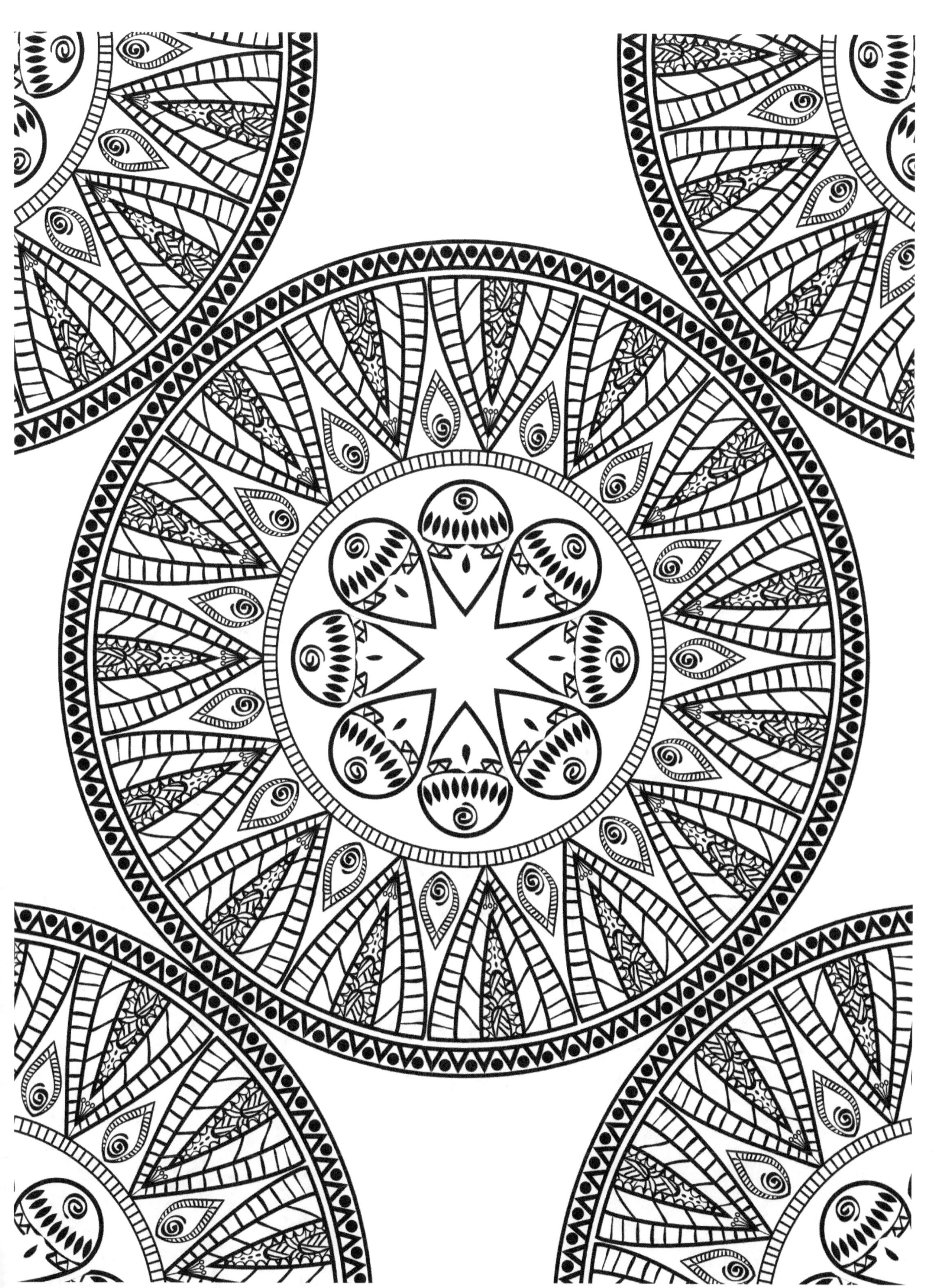

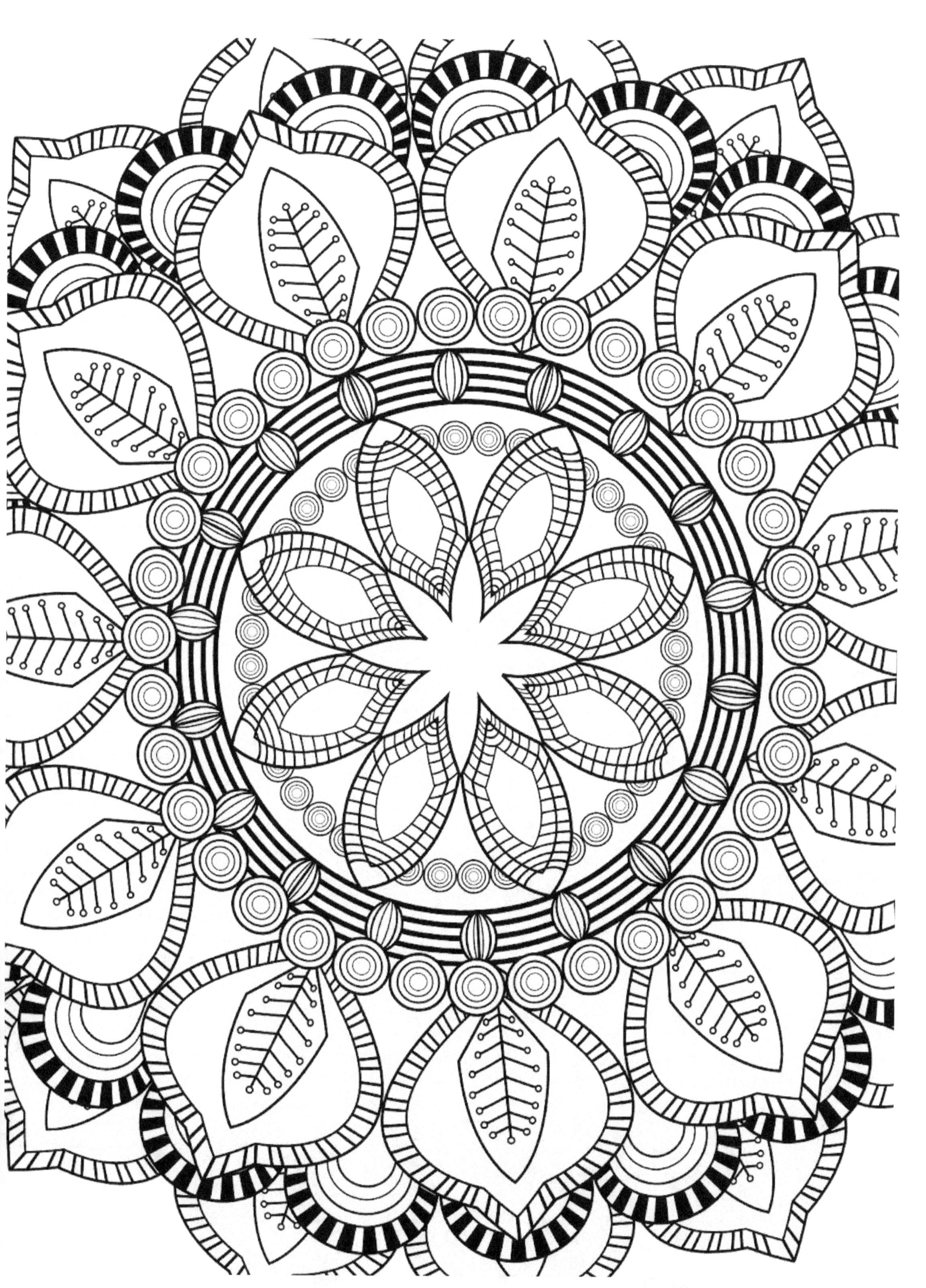

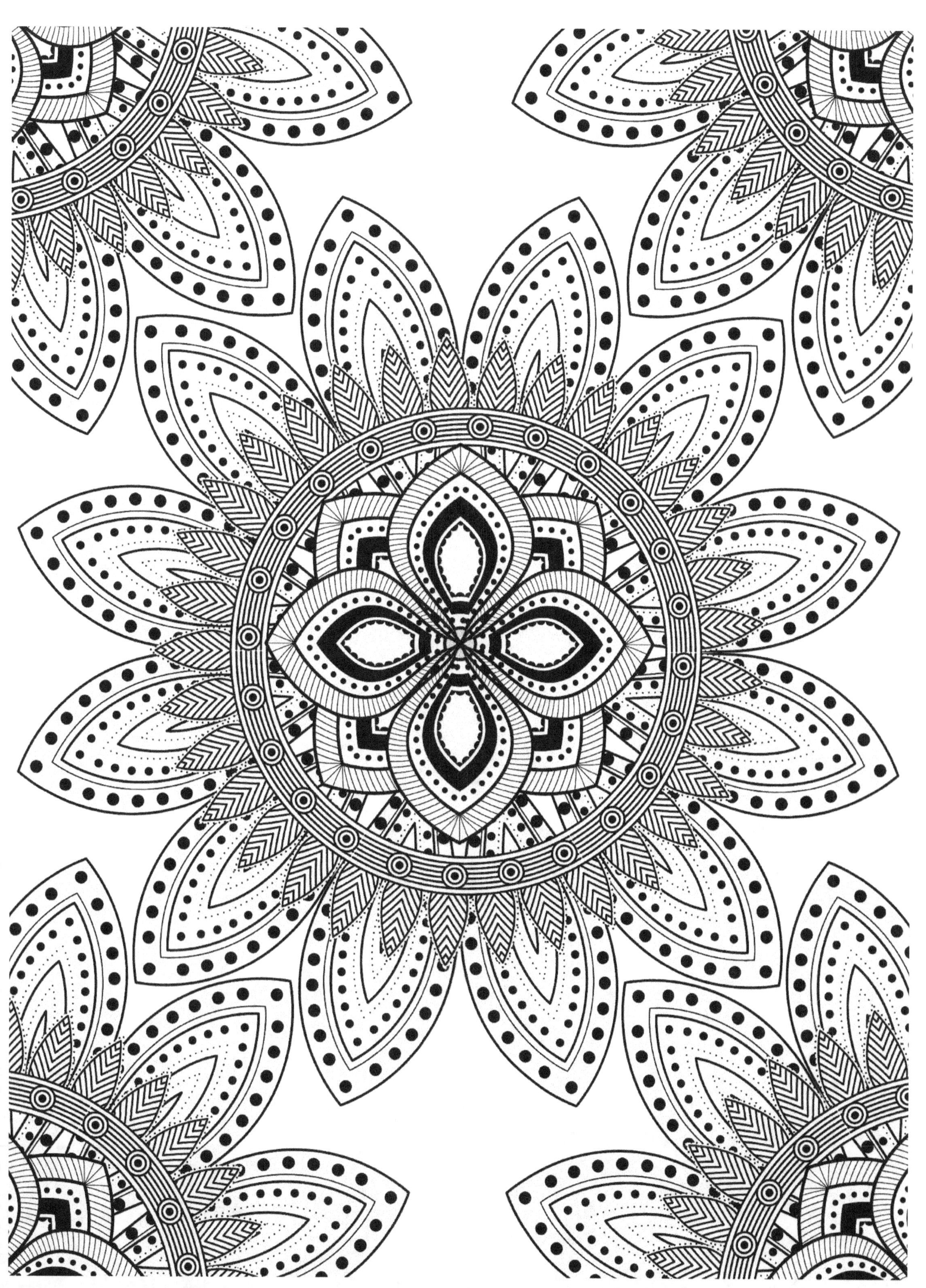

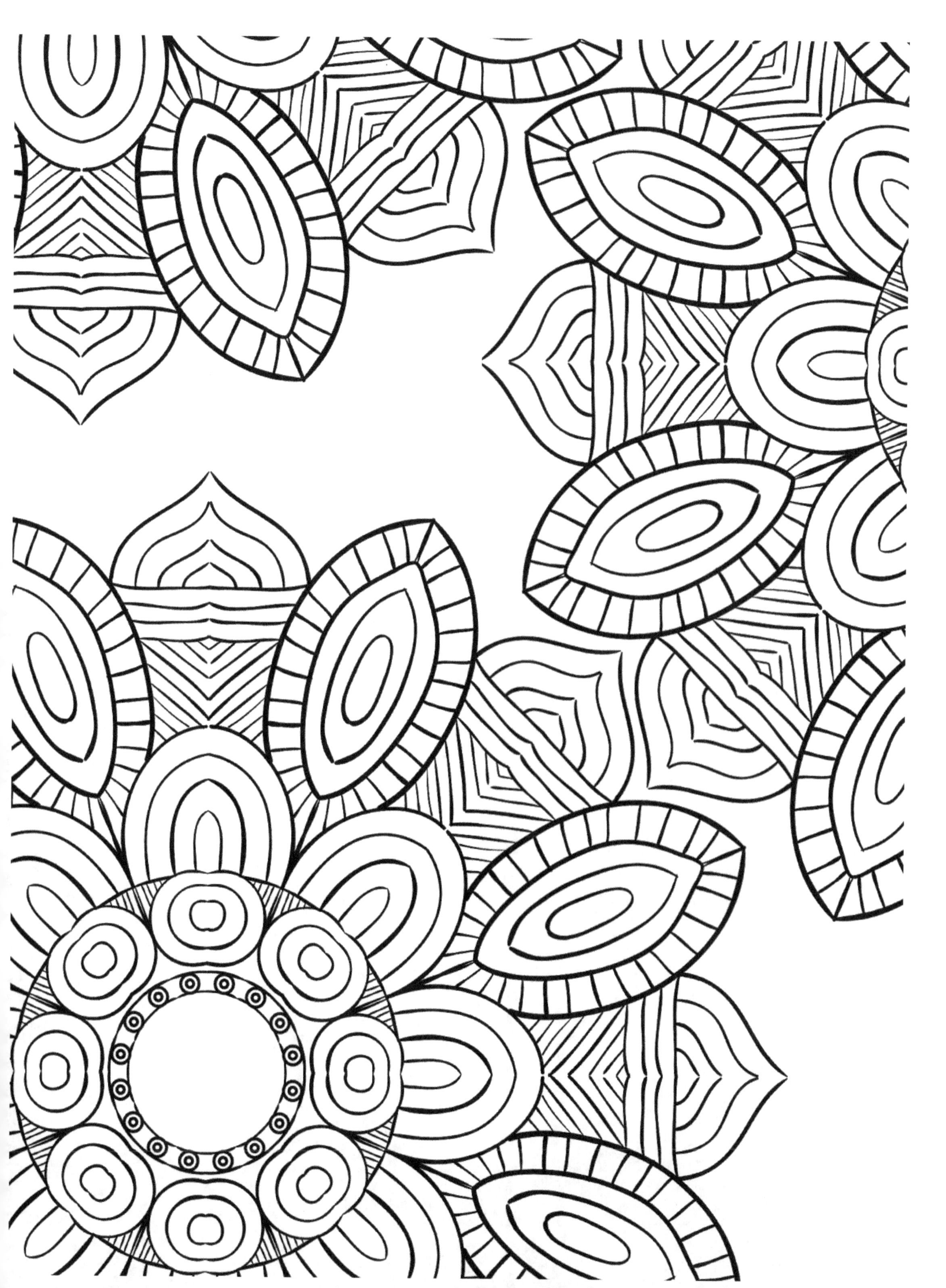

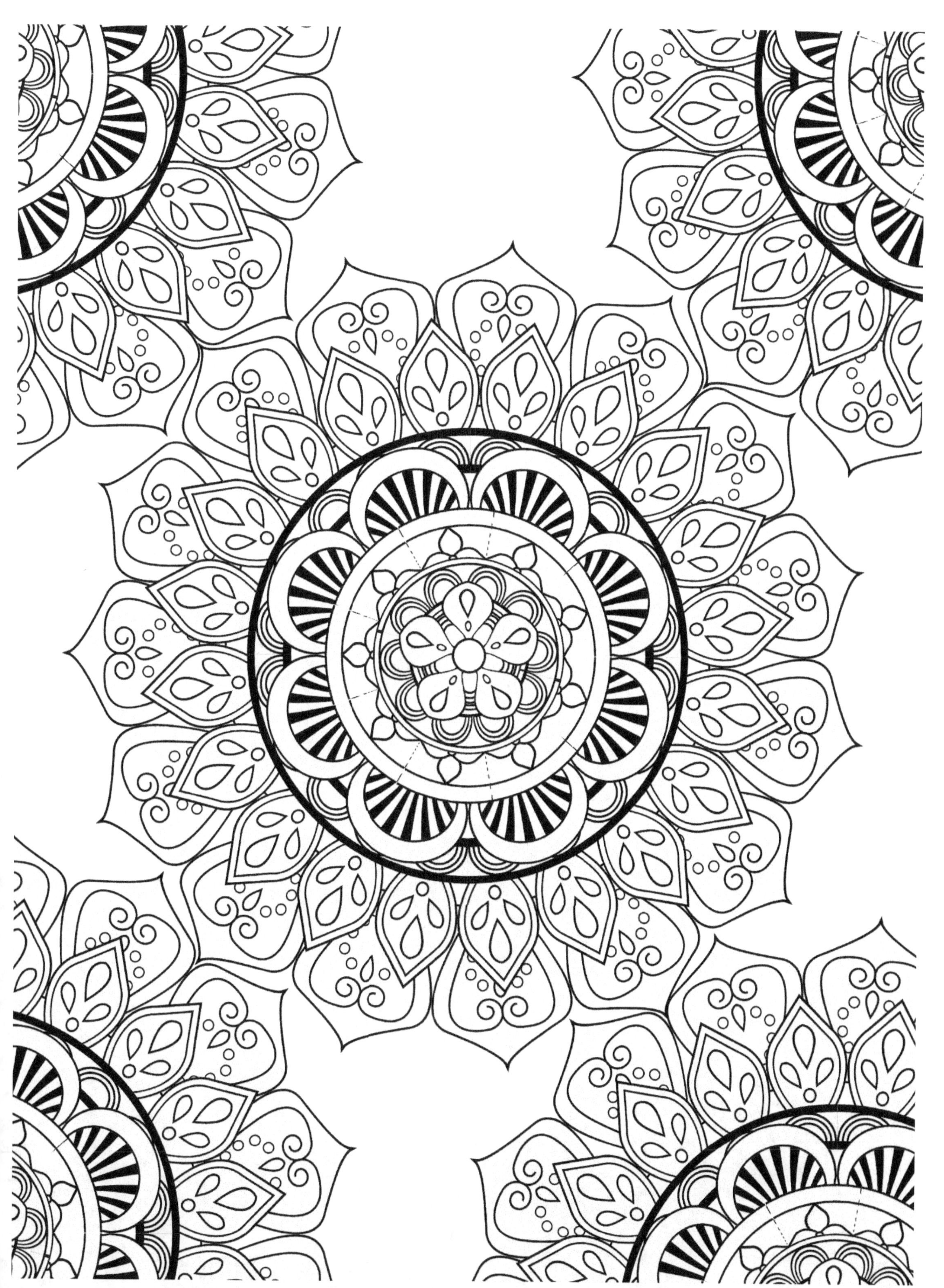

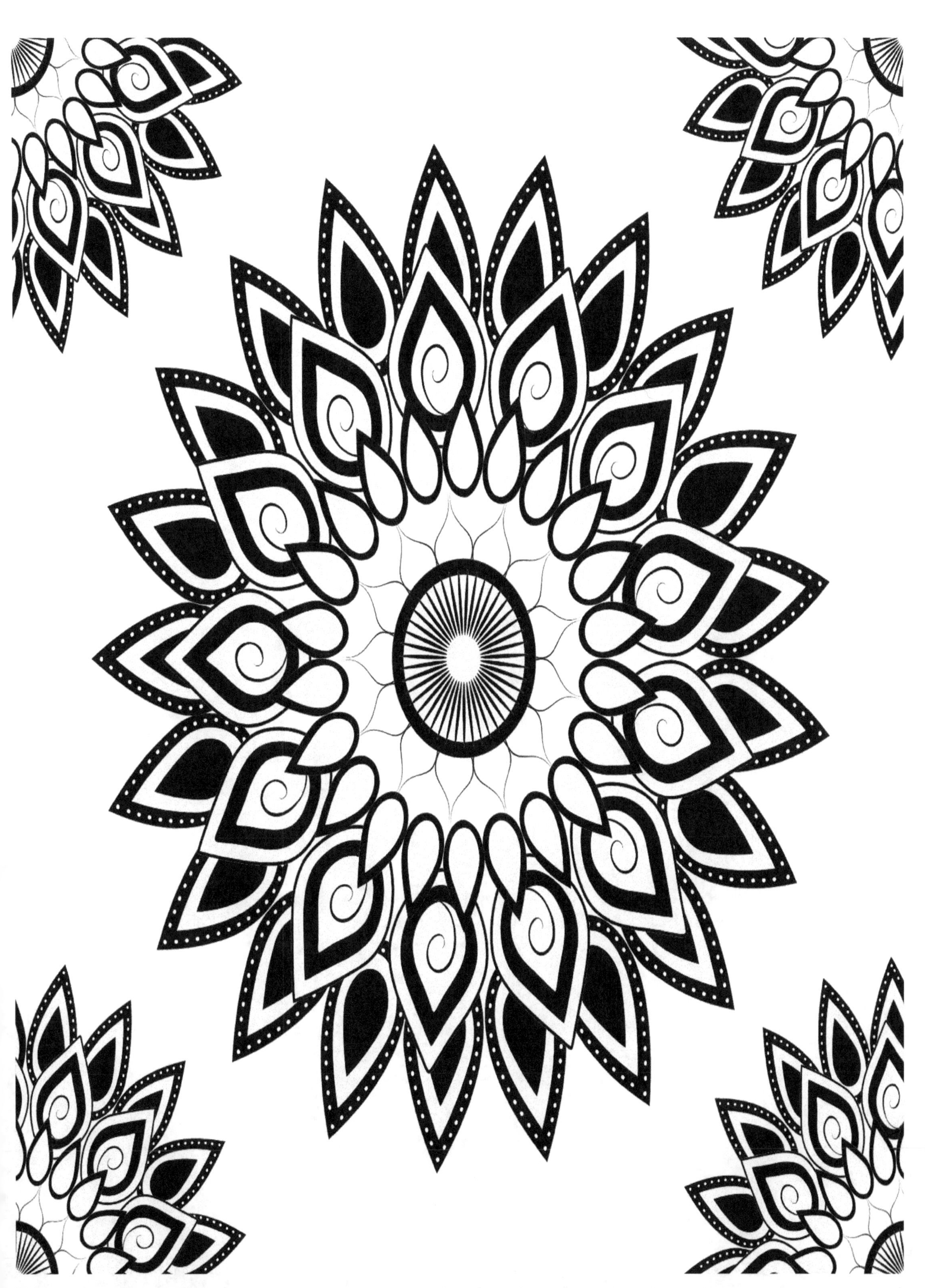

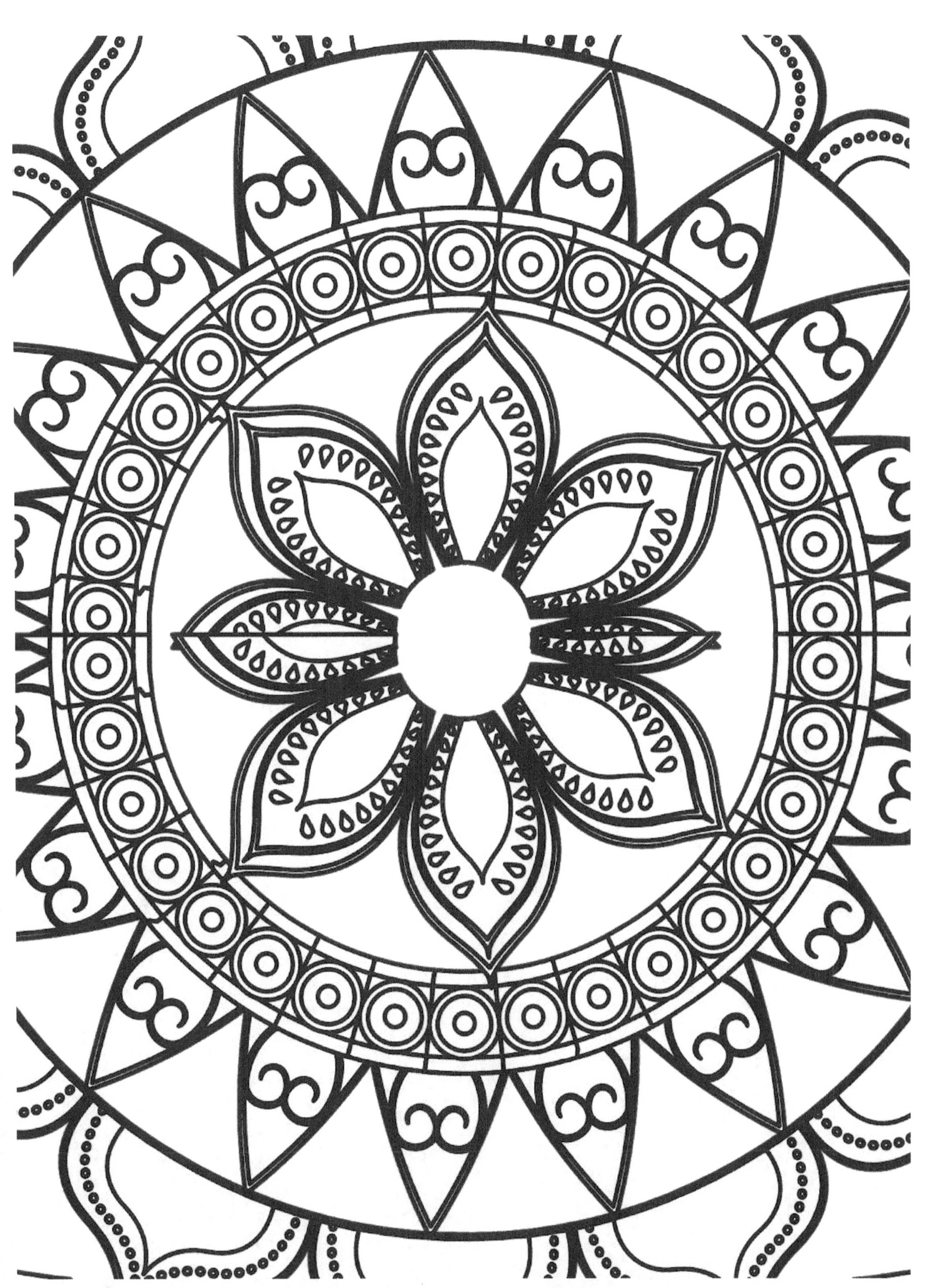

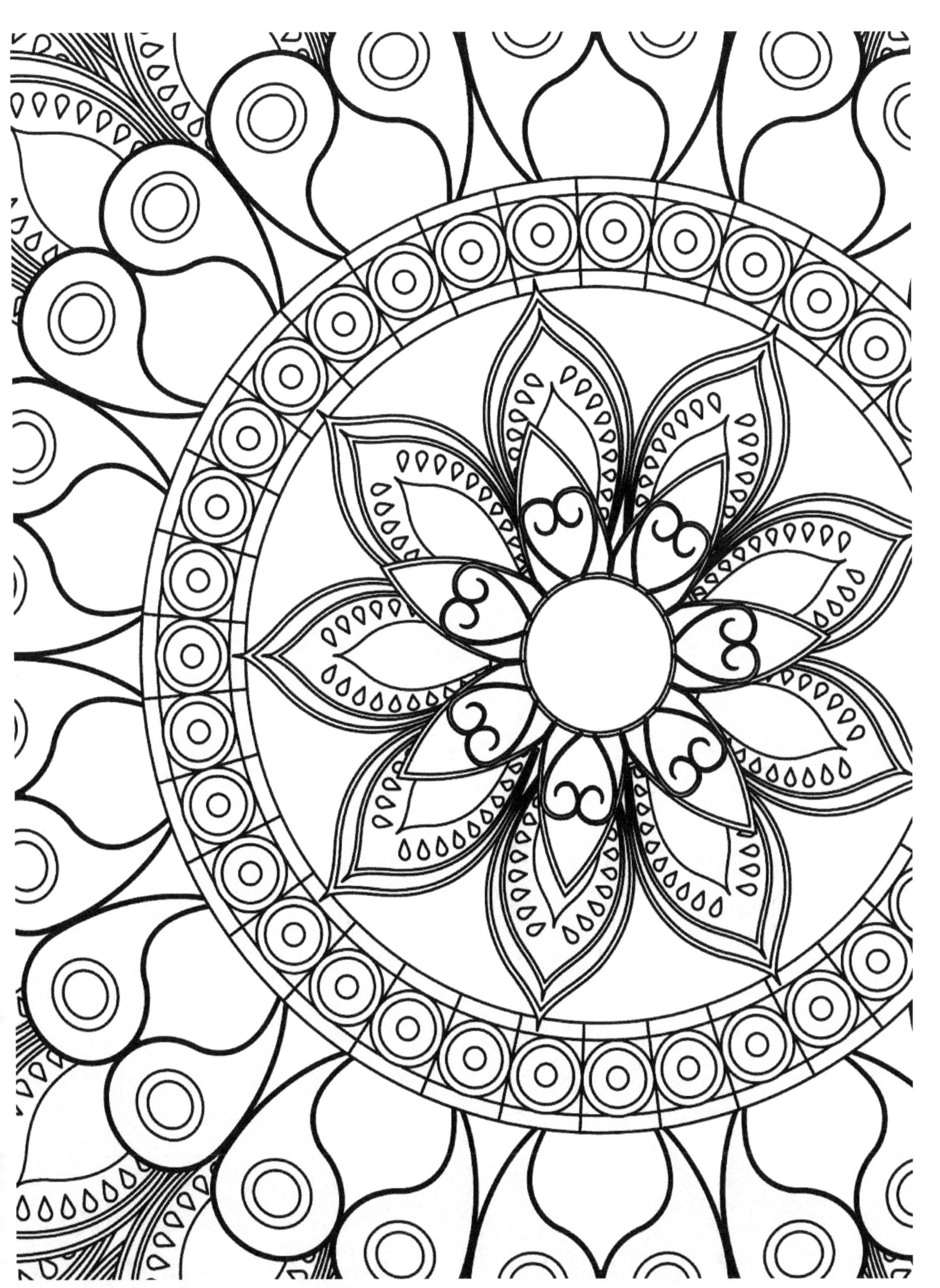

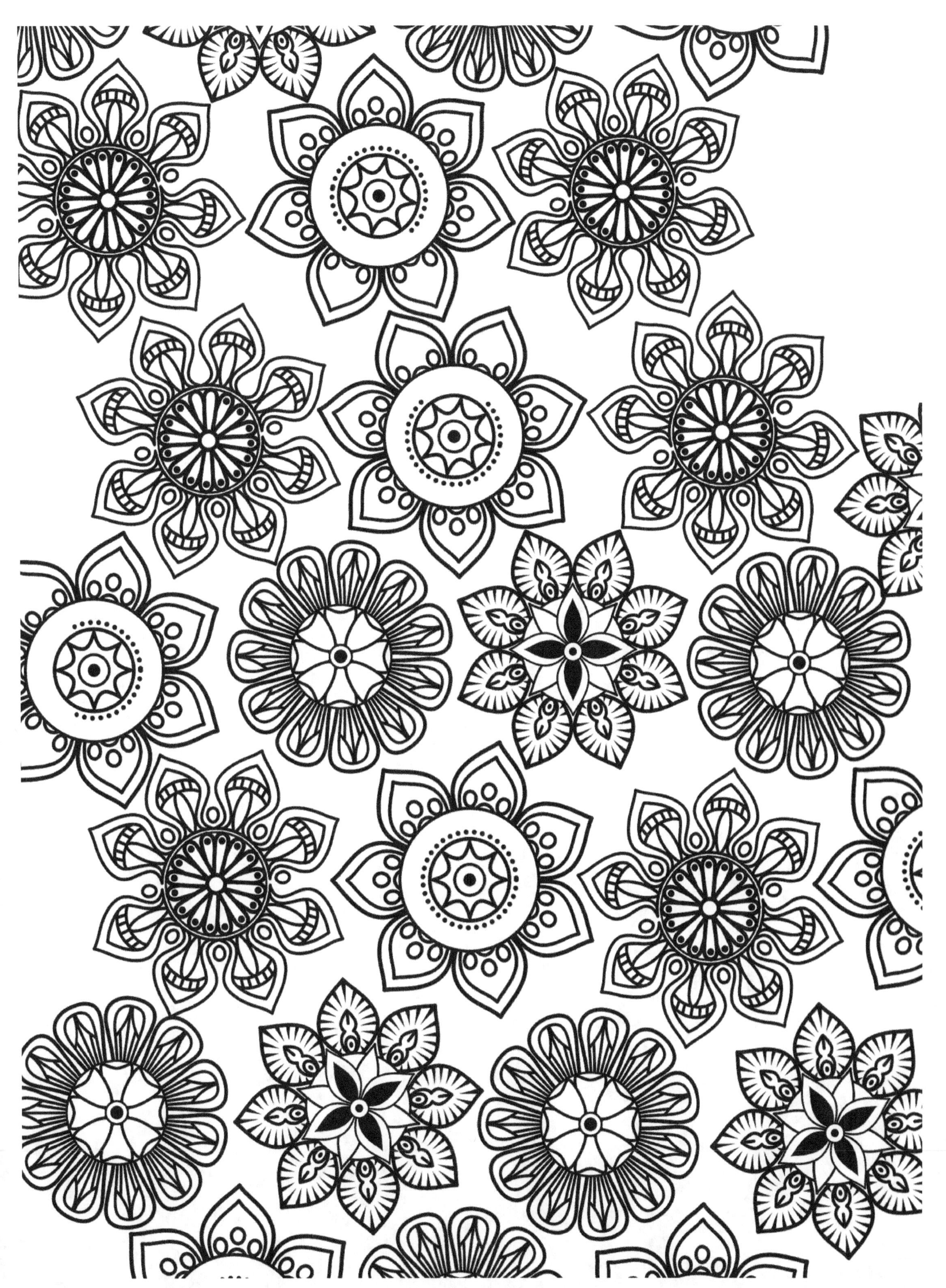

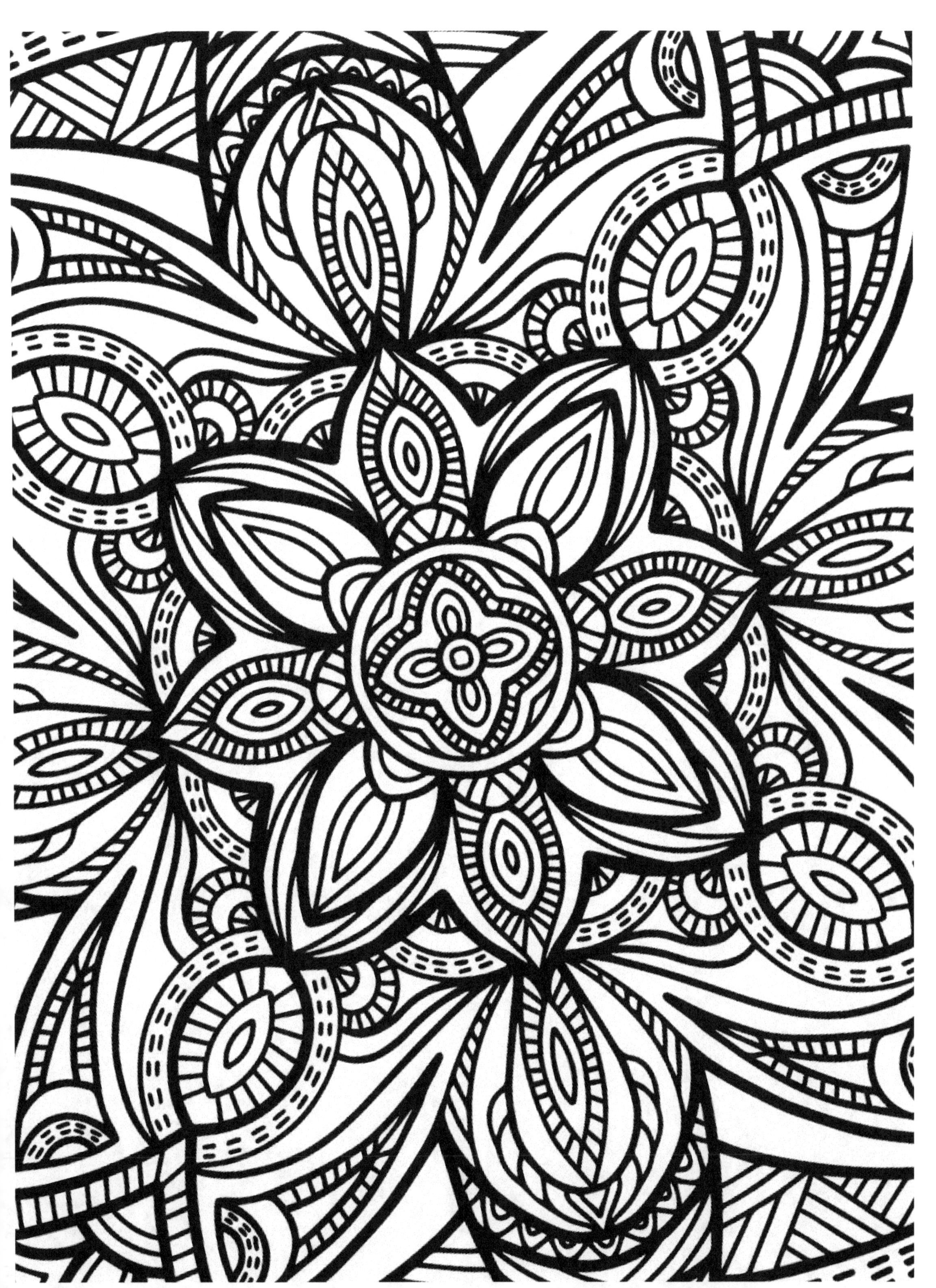

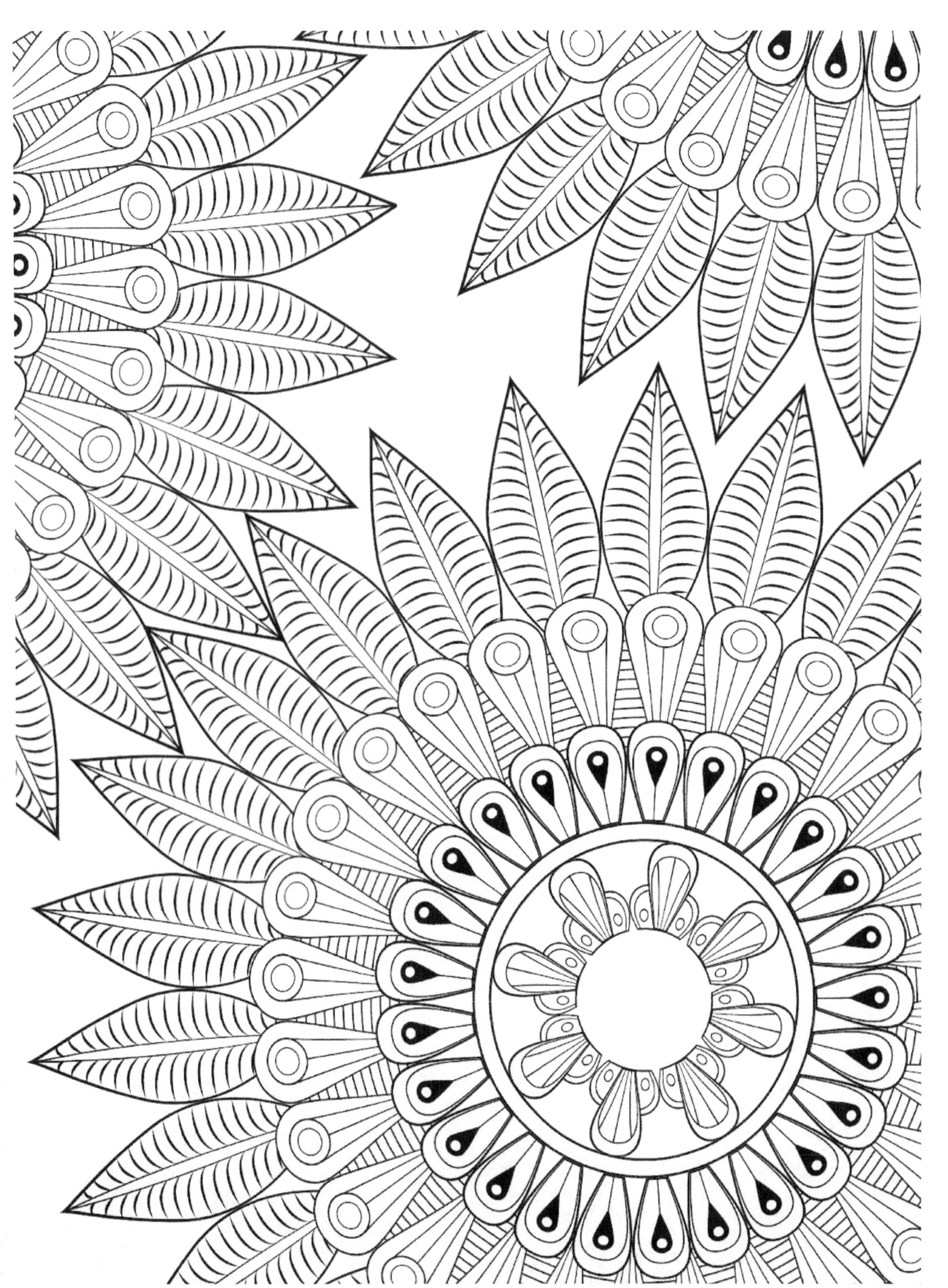

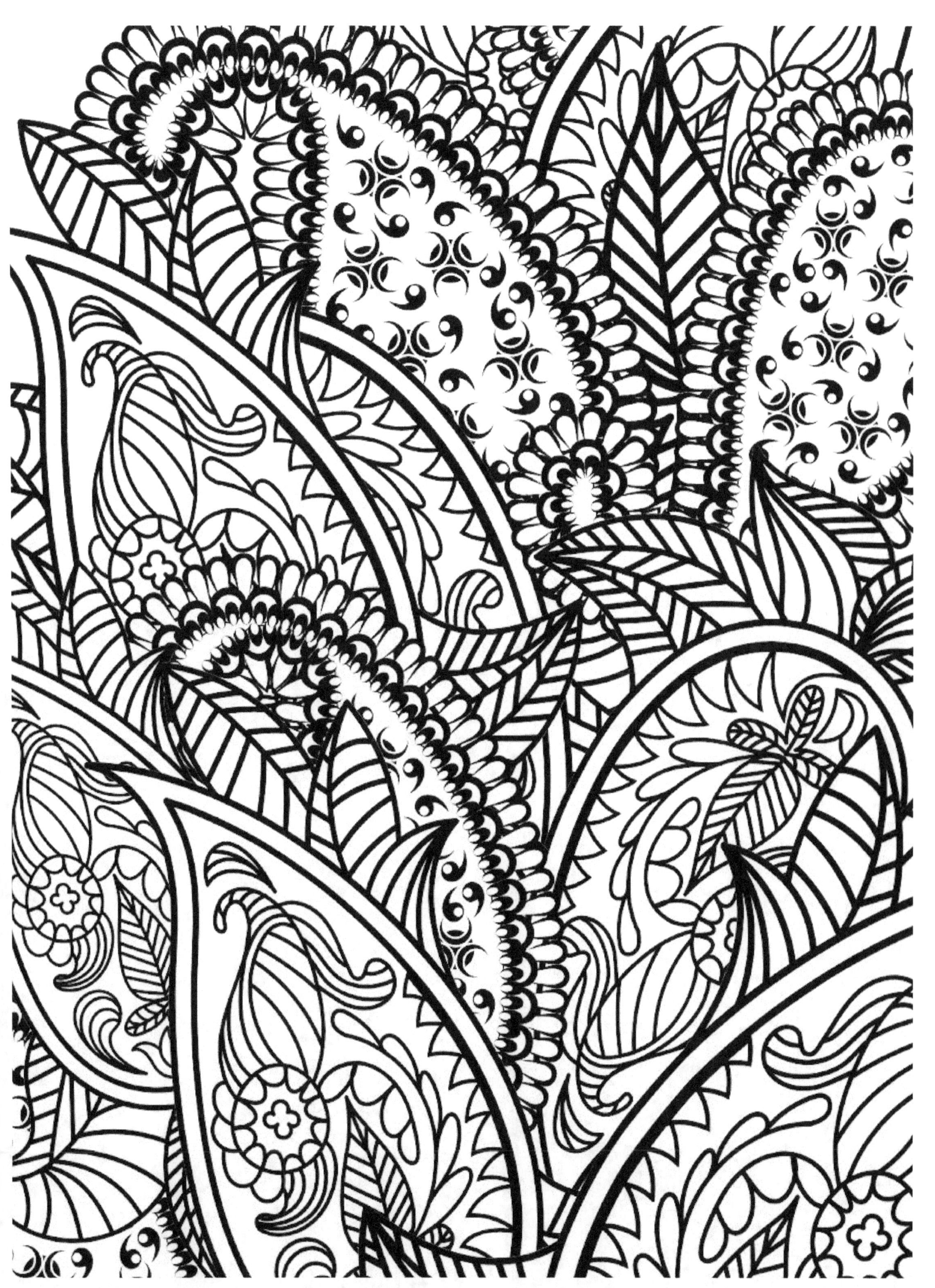

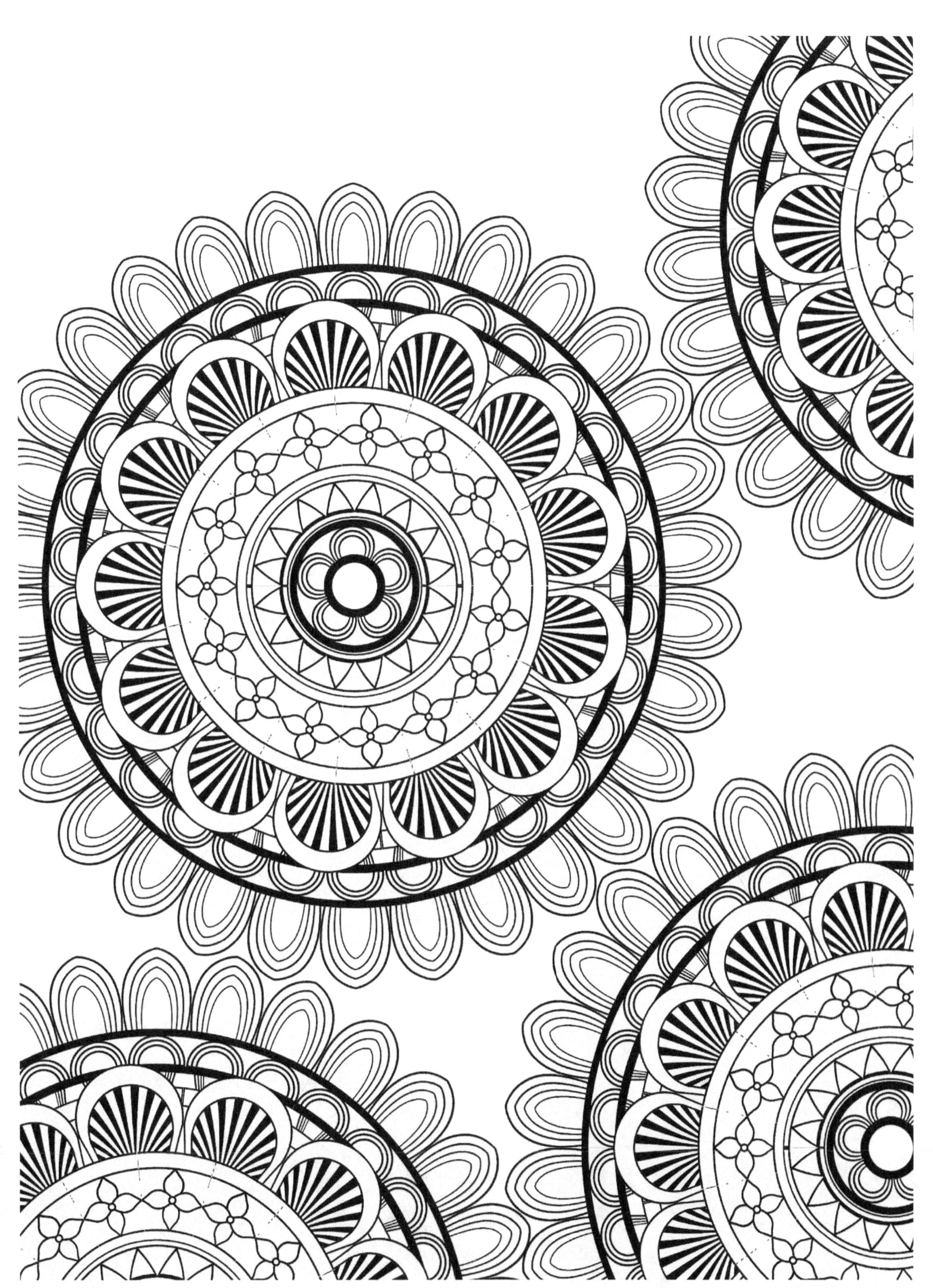

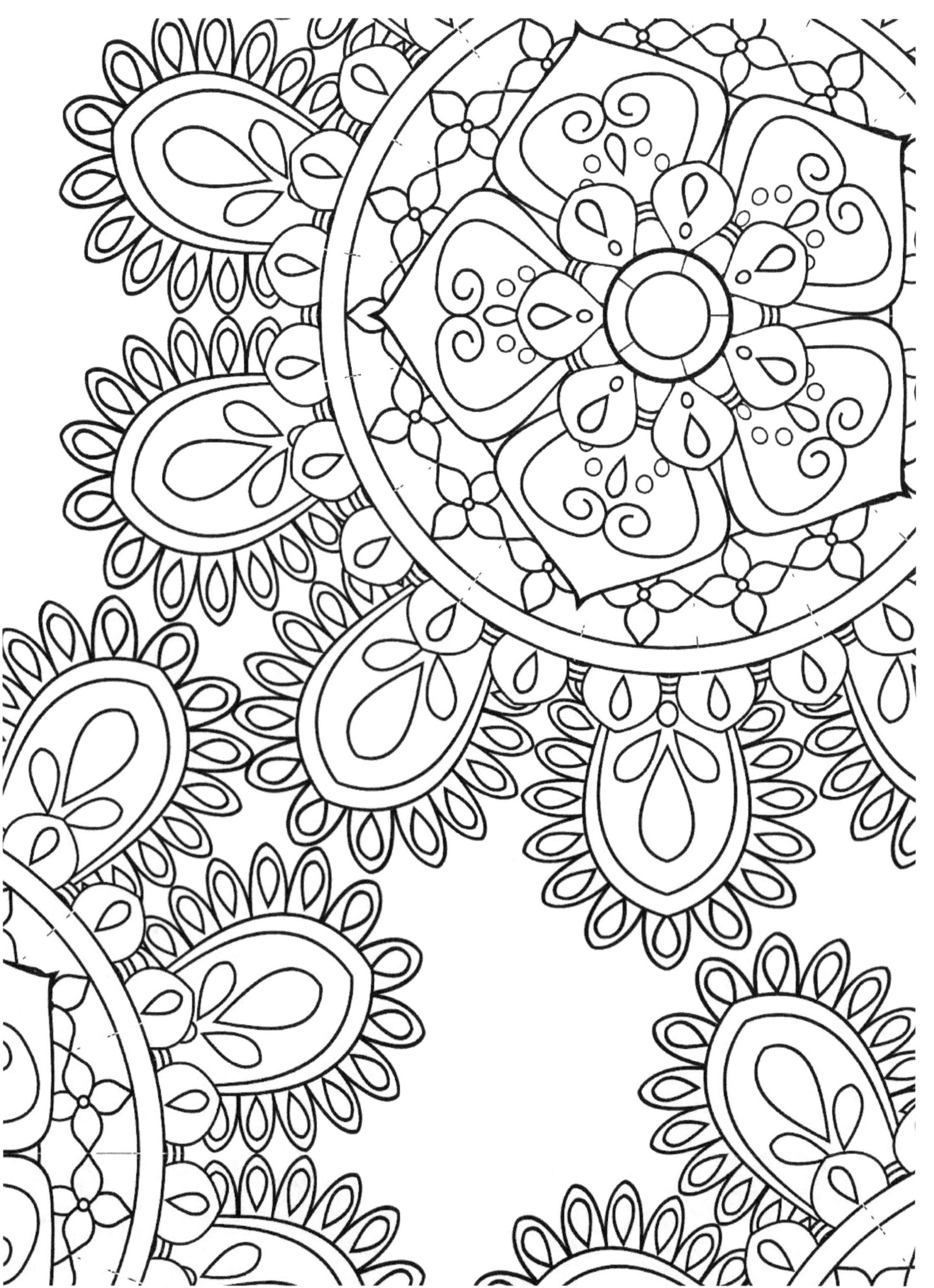

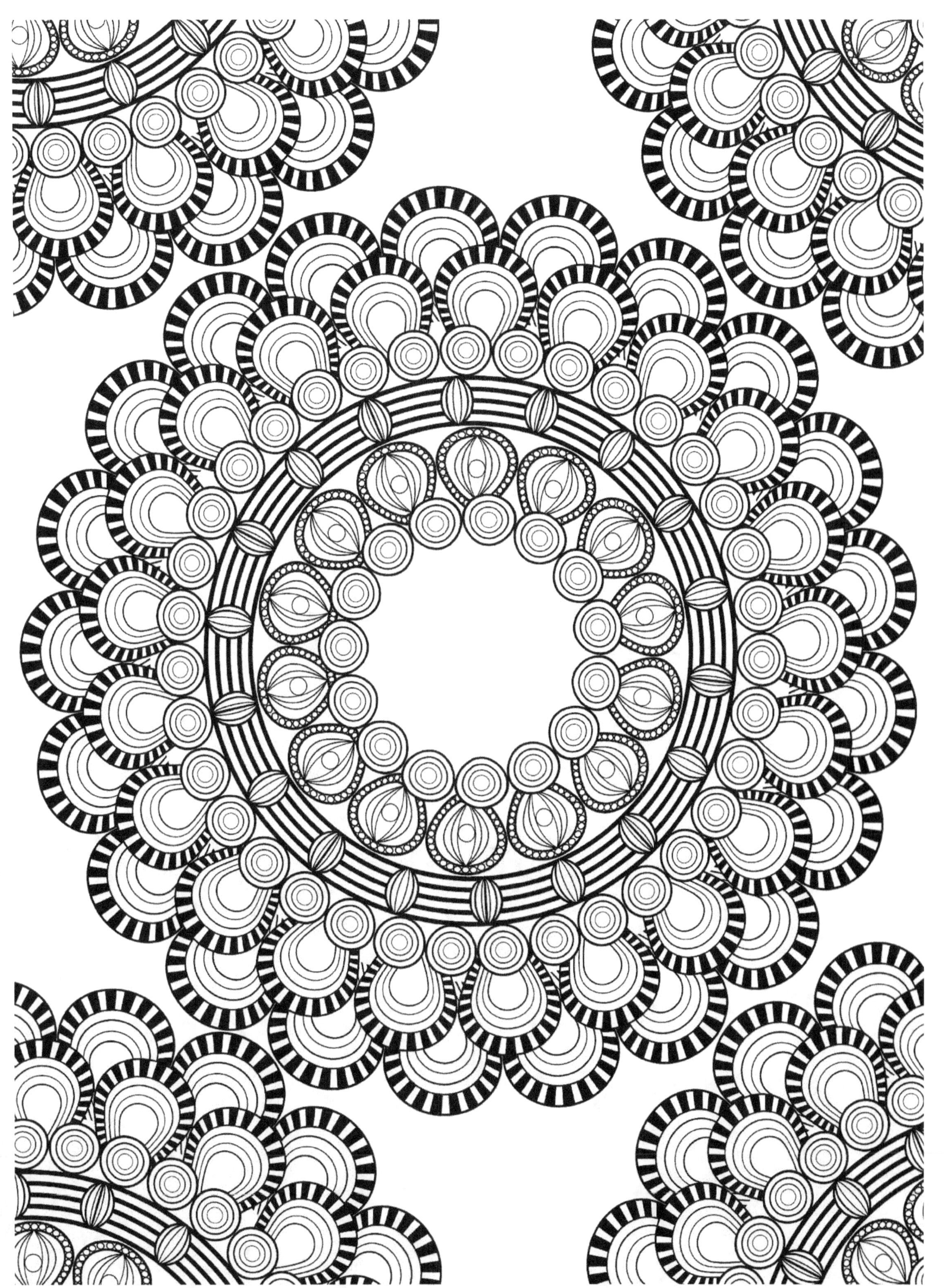

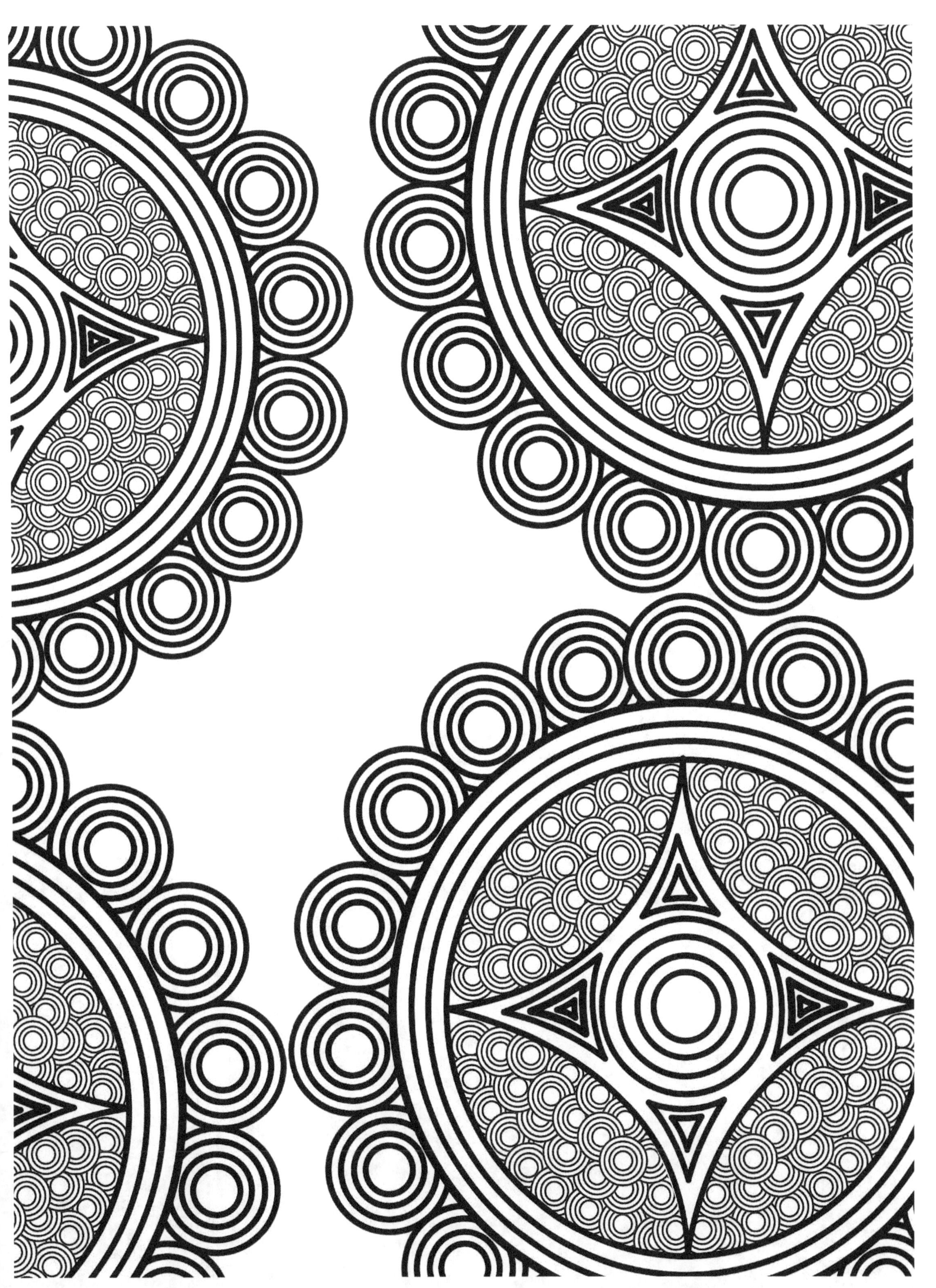

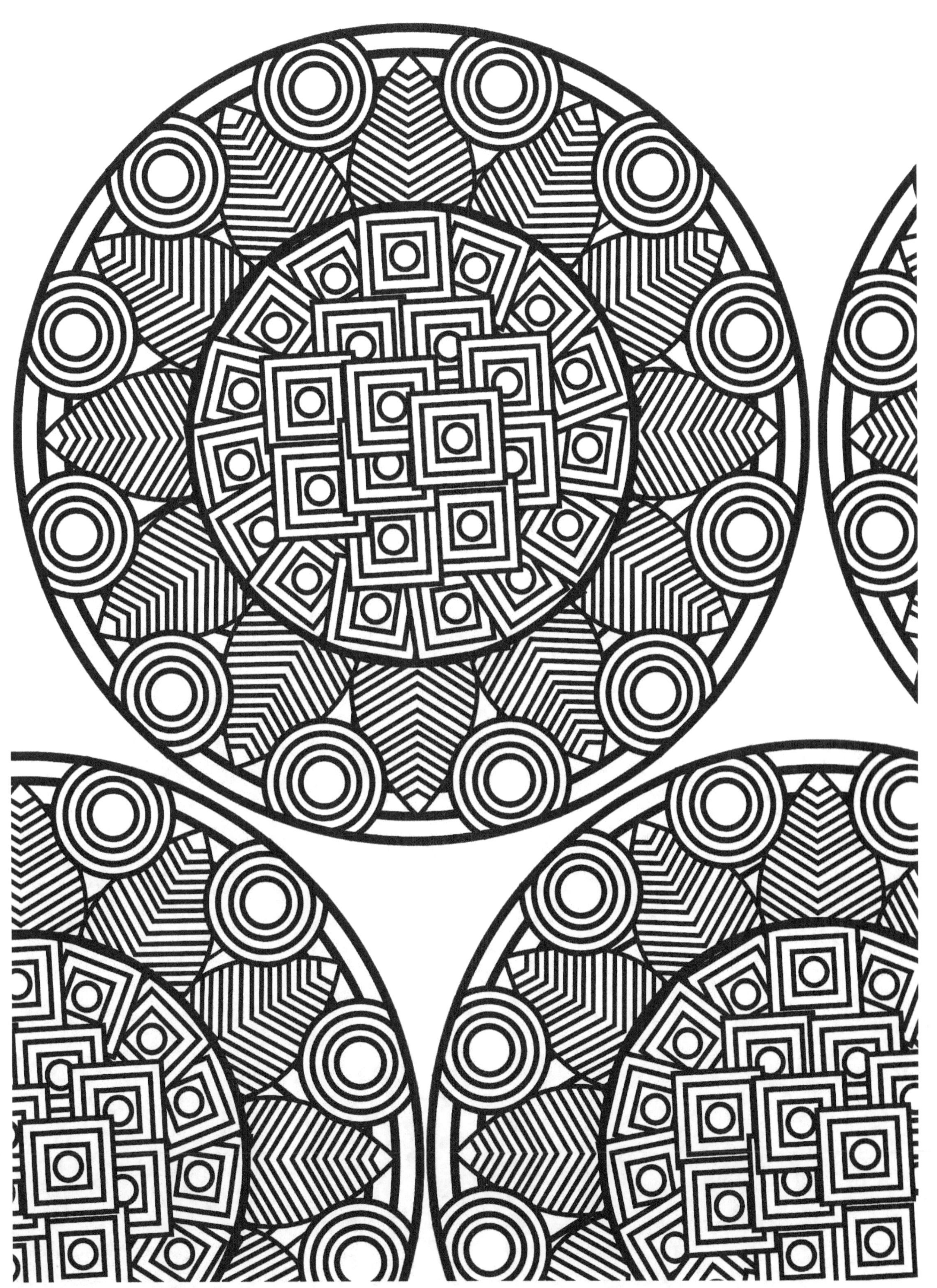

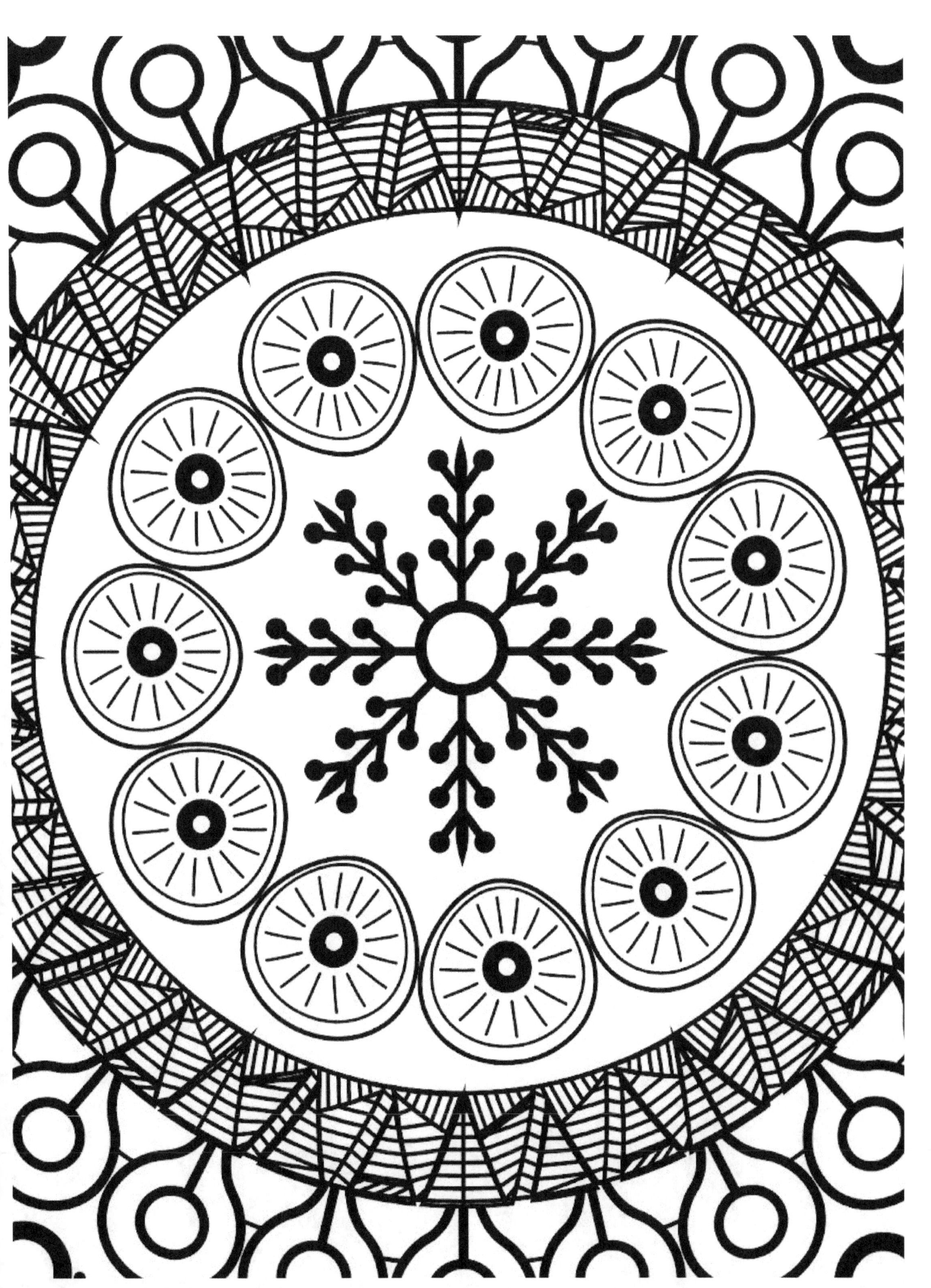

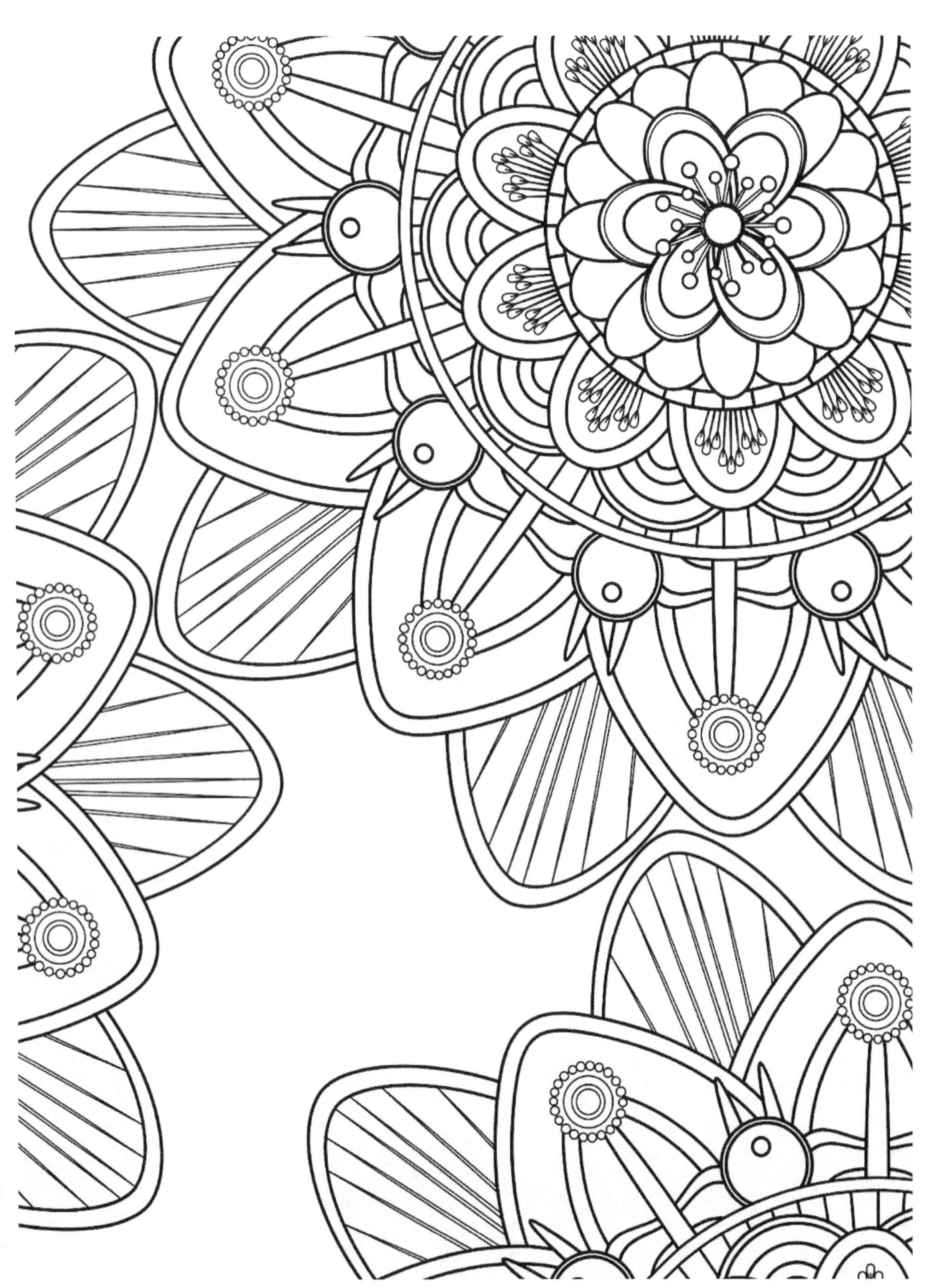

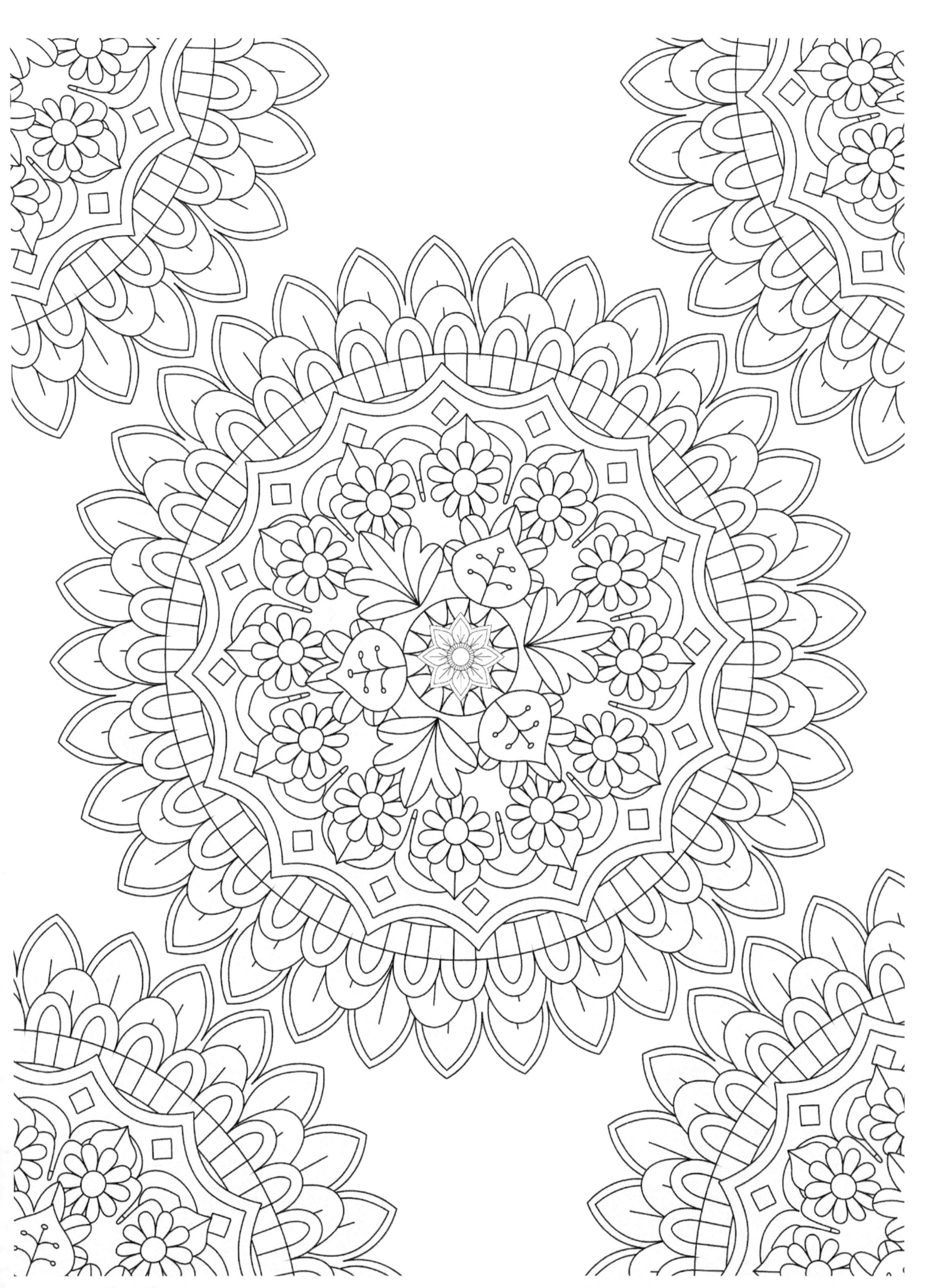

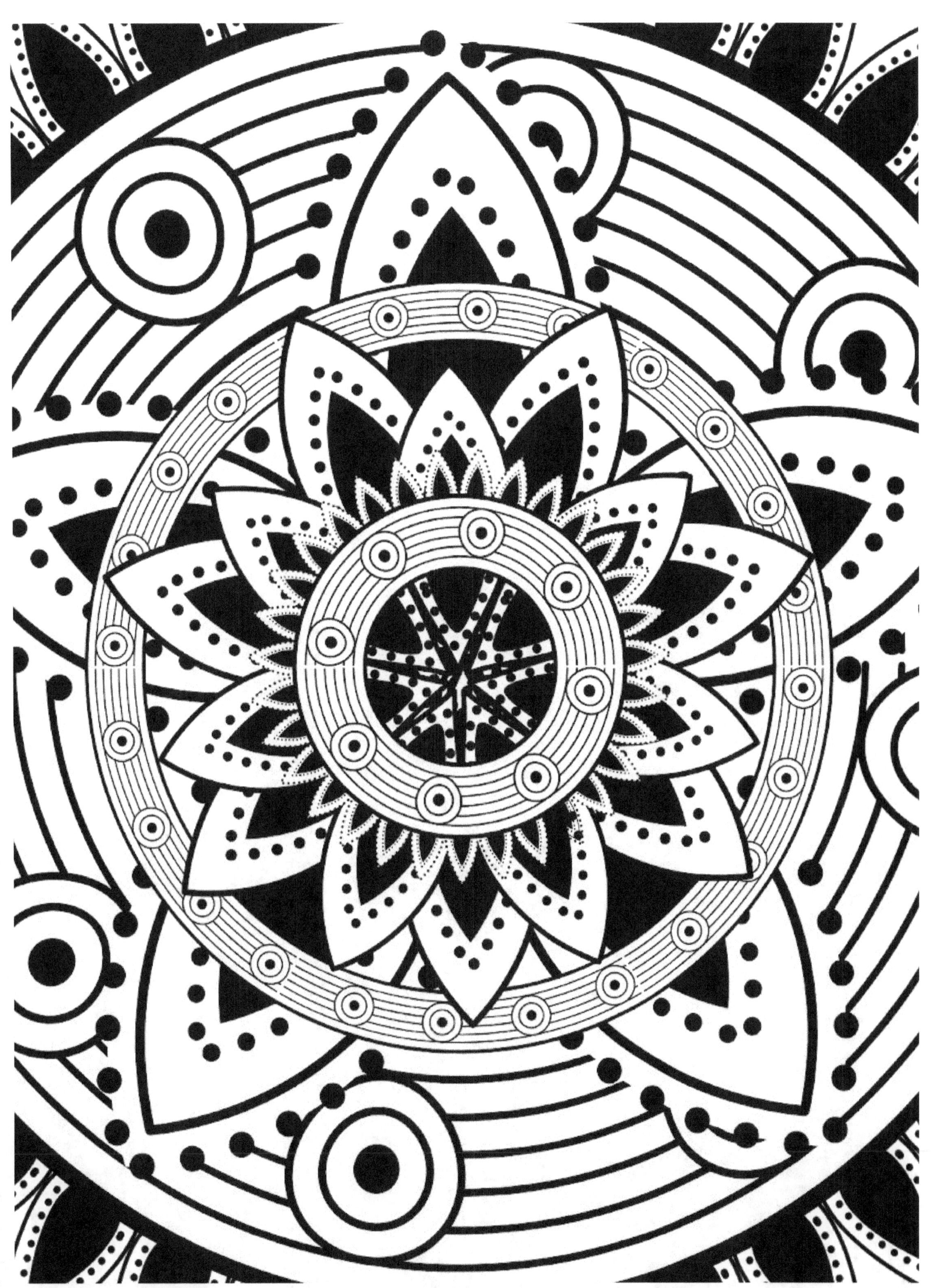

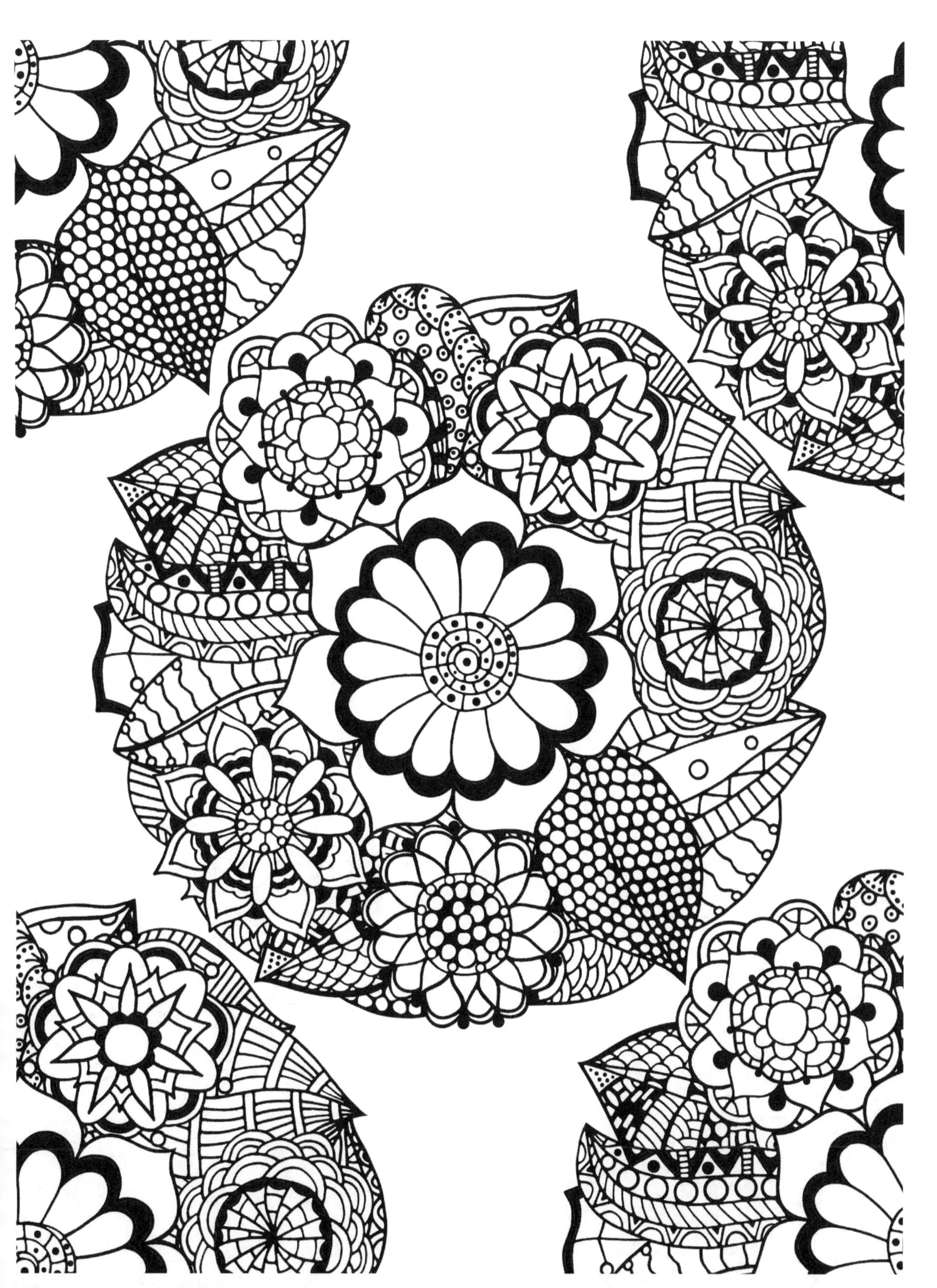

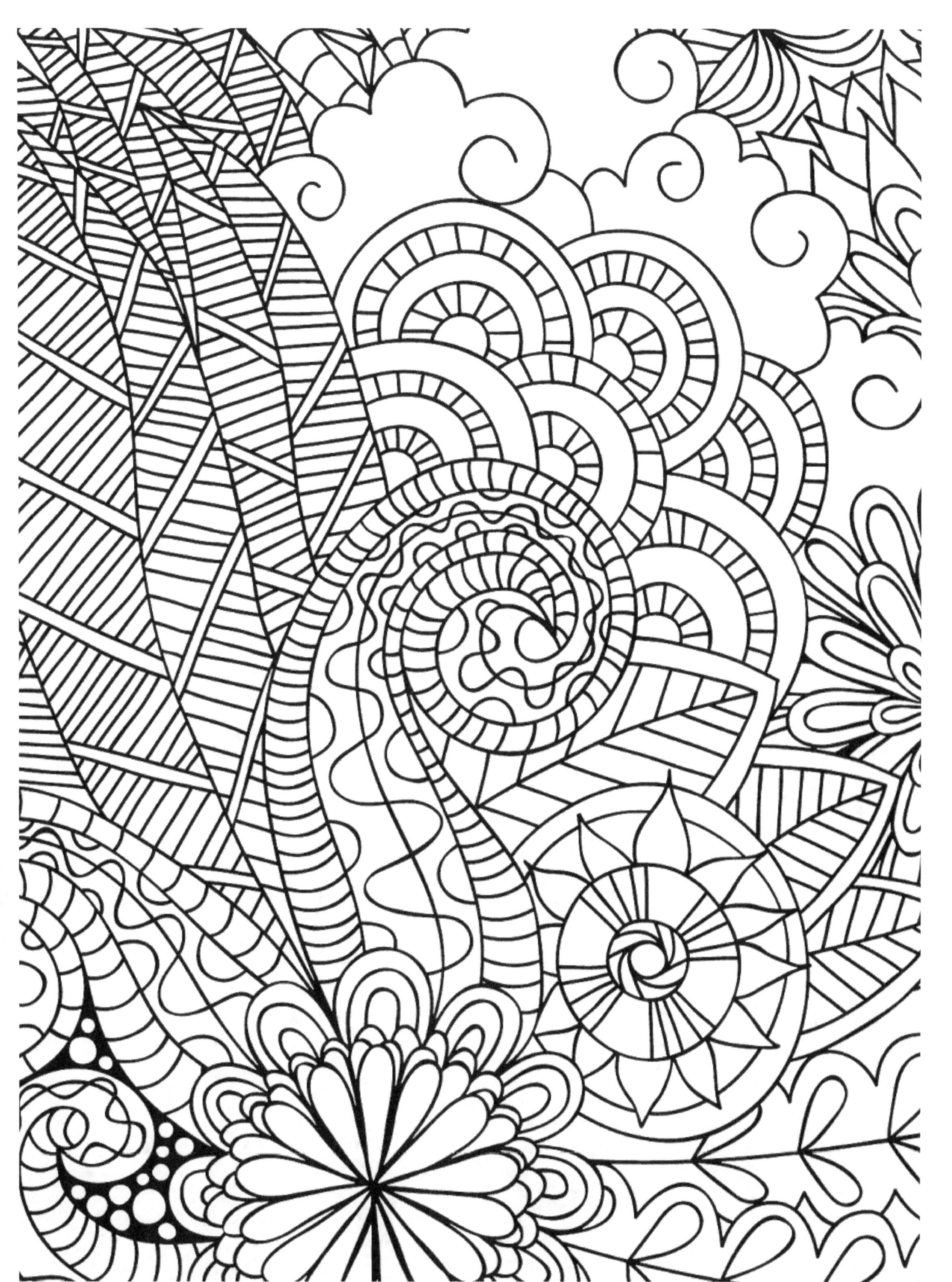

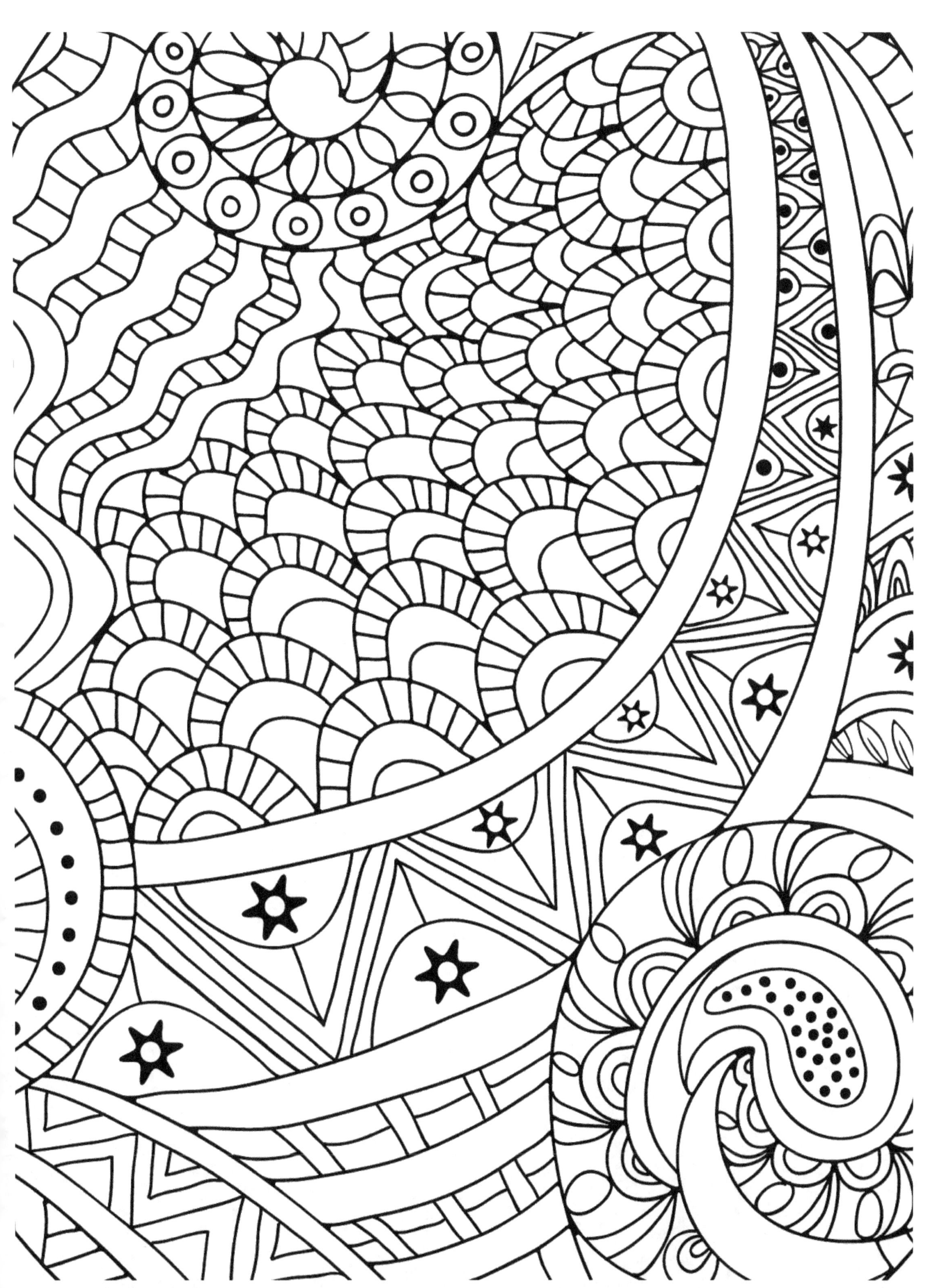

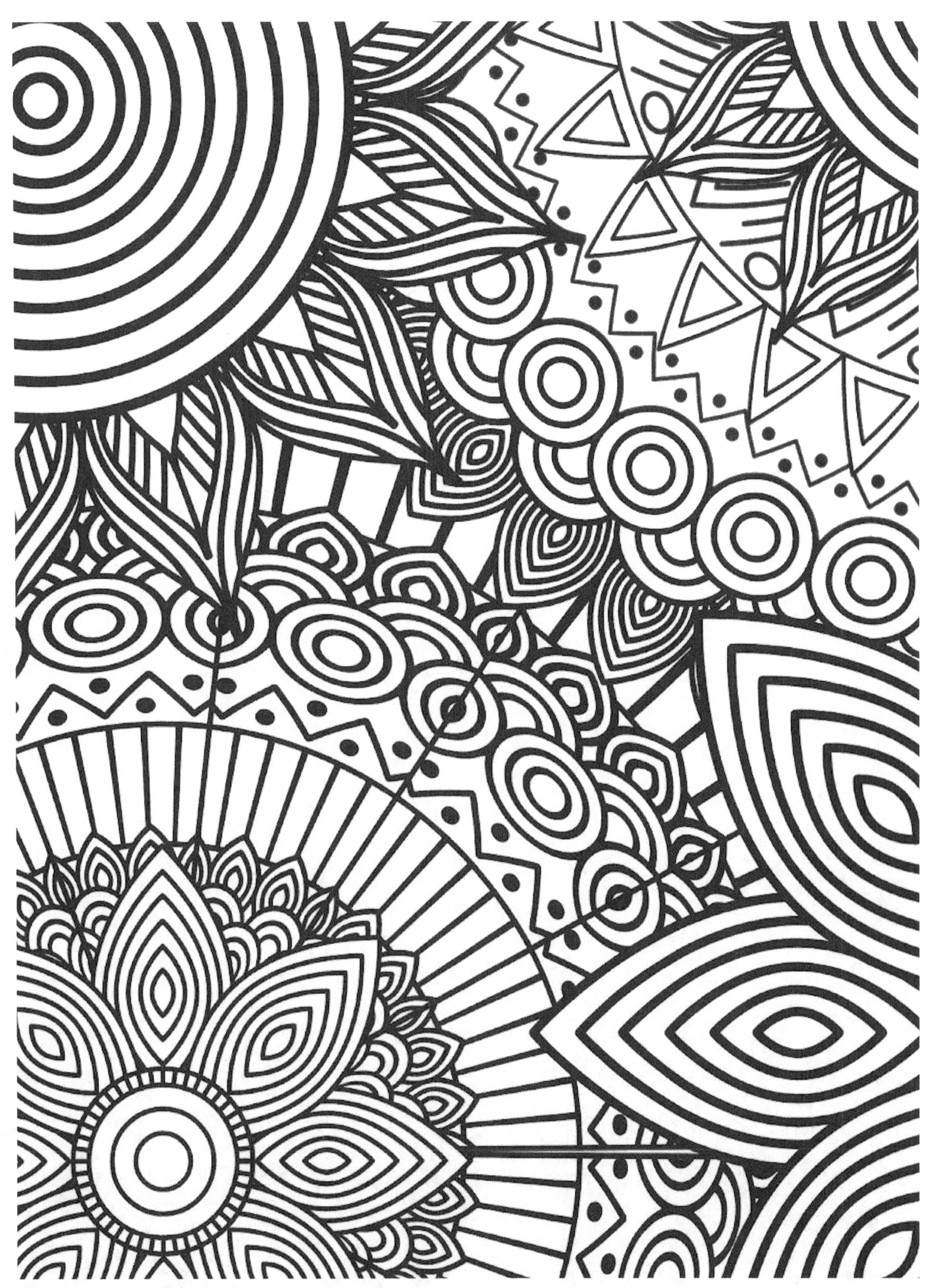

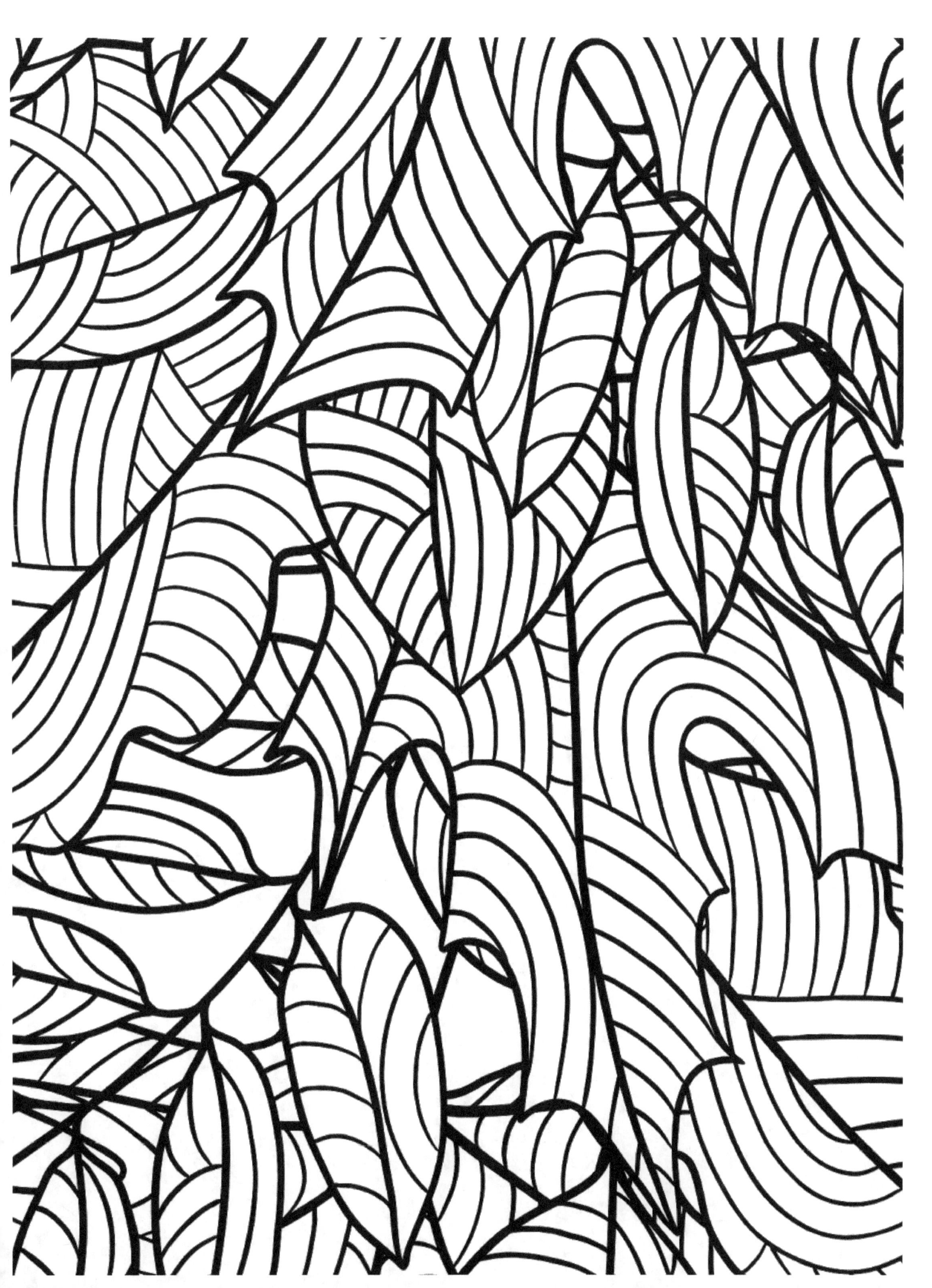

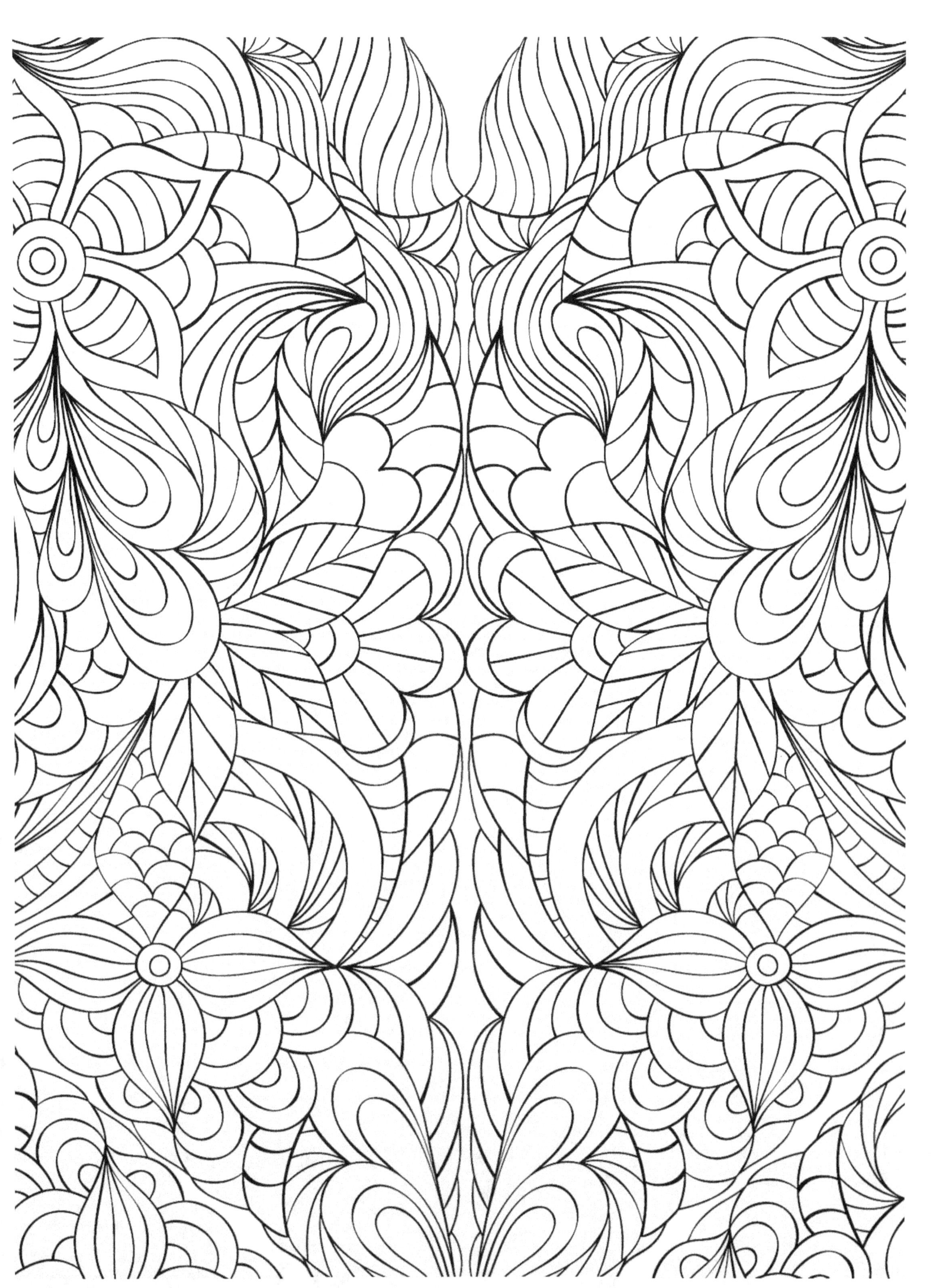

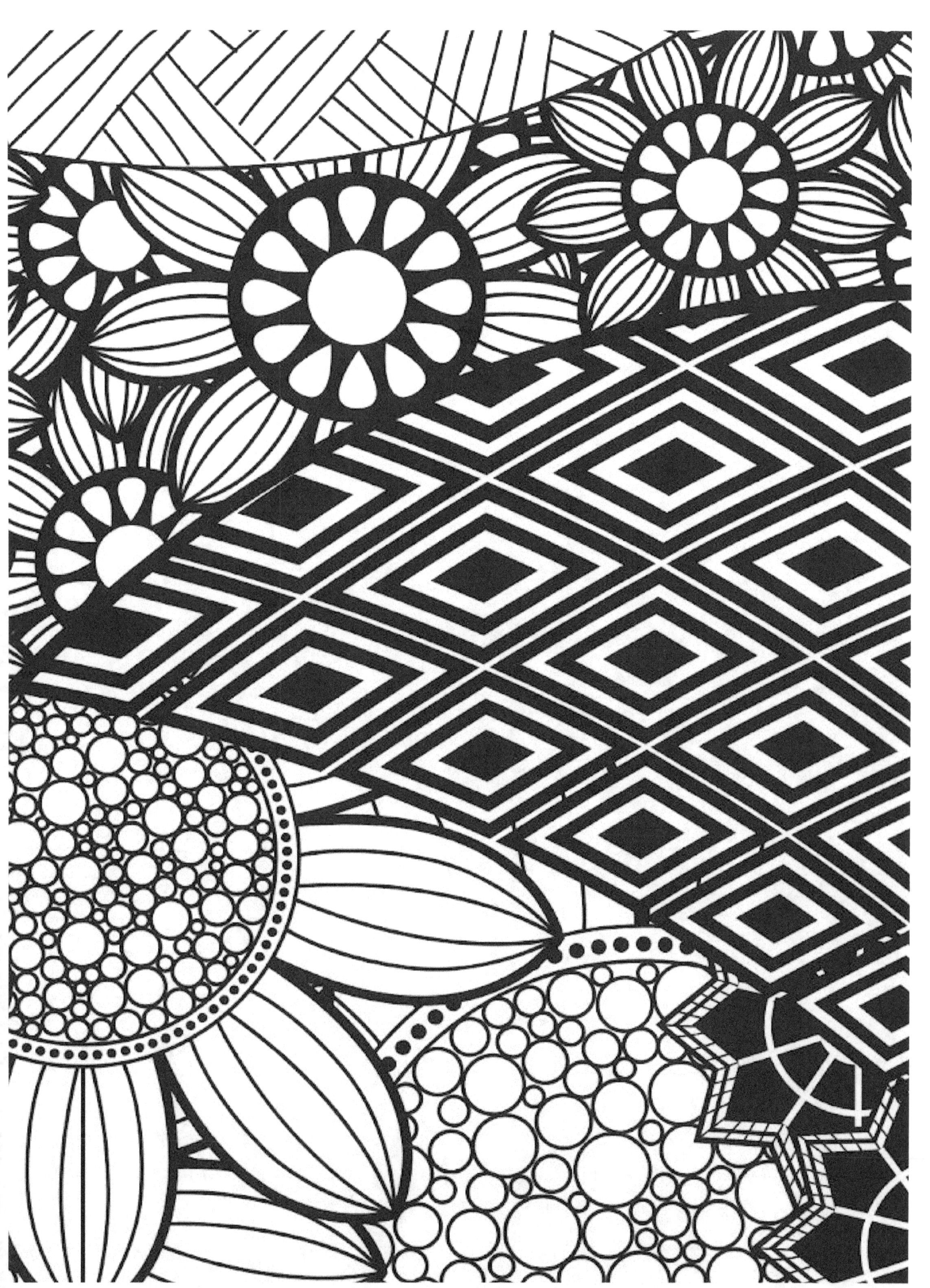

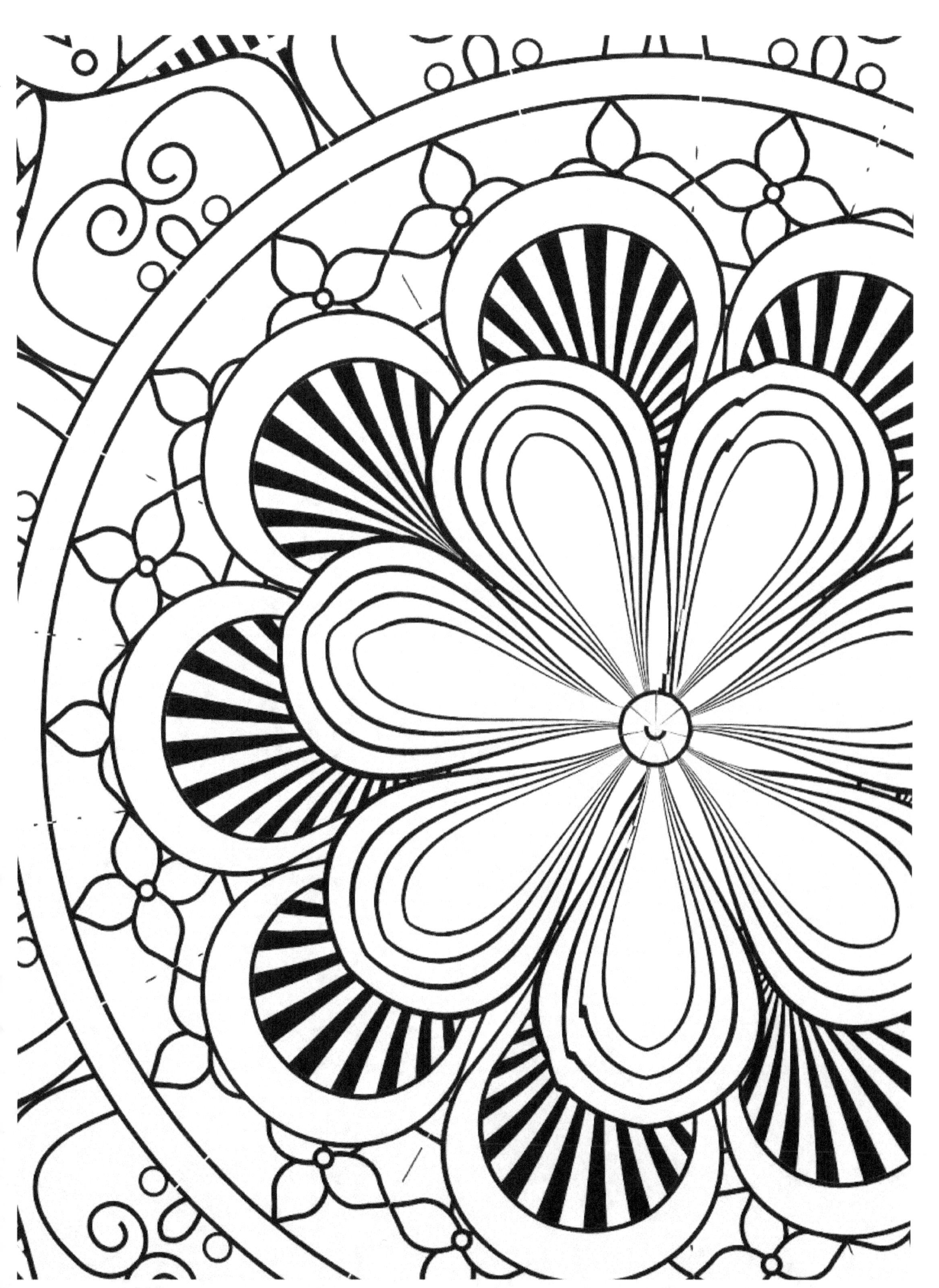

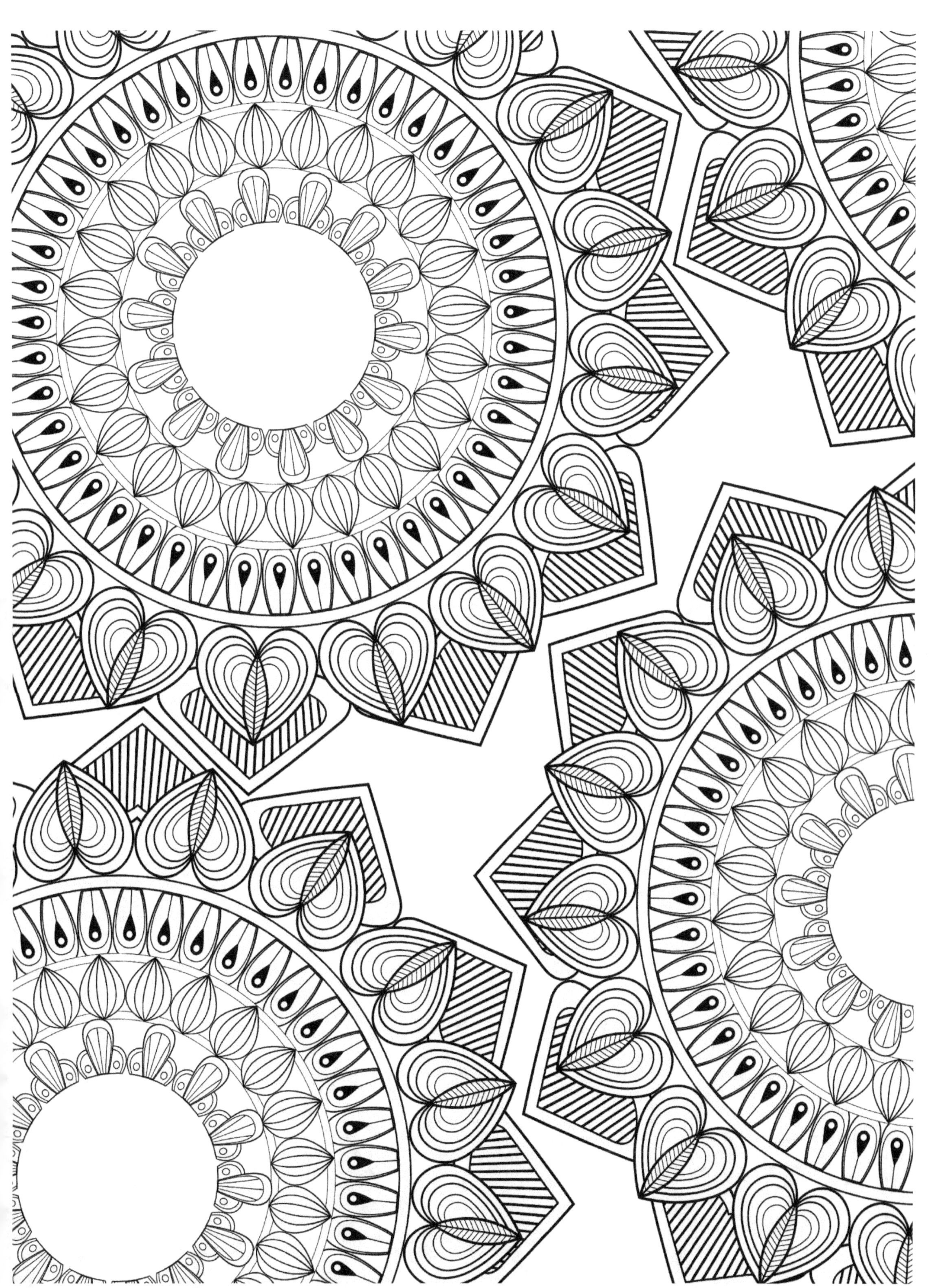

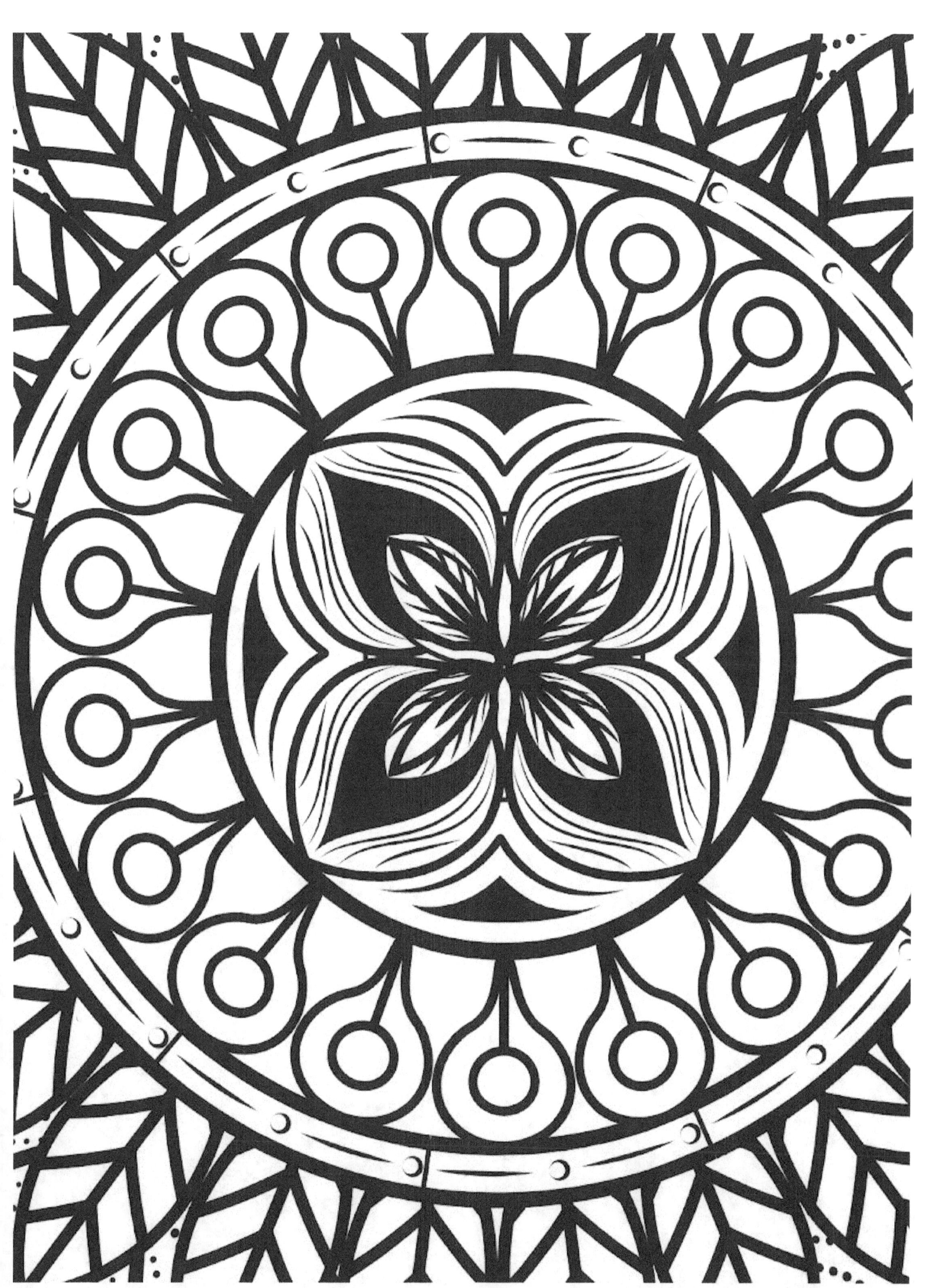